THE MEDITERRANEAN
DIET
Instant Pot Cookbook

Simplify Cooking and Eating
Delicious, Healthy, Quick and Easy Recipes

PETER BRAGG

Text Copyright © Peter Bragg

All rights reserved. No part of this guide may be reproduced in any form without permission in writing from the publisher except in the case of brief quotations embodied in critical articles or reviews.

Legal & Disclaimer

The information contained in this book and its contents is not designed to replace or take the place of any form of medical or professional advice; and is not meant to replace the need for independent medical, financial, legal or other professional advice or services, as may be required. The content and information in this book has been provided for educational and entertainment purposes only.

The content and information contained in this book has been compiled from sources deemed reliable, and it is accurate to the best of the Author's knowledge, information and belief. However, the Author cannot guarantee its accuracy and validity and cannot be held liable for any errors and/or omissions. Further, changes are periodically made to this book as and when needed. Where appropriate and/or necessary, you must consult a professional (including but not limited to your doctor, attorney, financial advisor or such other professional advisor) before using any of the suggested remedies, techniques, or information in this book.

Upon using the contents and information contained in this book, you agree to hold harmless the Author from and against any damages, costs, and expenses, including any legal fees potentially resulting from the application of any of the information provided by this book. This disclaimer applies to any loss, damages or injury caused by the use and application, whether directly or indirectly, of any advice or information presented, whether for breach of contract, tort, negligence, personal injury, criminal intent, or under any other cause of action.

You agree to accept all risks of using the information presented inside this book.

You agree that by continuing to read this book, where appropriate and/or necessary, you shall consult a professional (including but not limited to your doctor, attorney, or financial advisor or such other advisor as needed) before using any of the suggested remedies, techniques, or information in this book.

Table of Contents

7

Description

Hello! Welcome to the book of THE MEDITERRANEAN DIET Instant Pot Cookbook. The recipes are simply too delicious to keep to oneself., and it's the only cookbook you'll need to make the most delicious Instant Pot recipes you've ever tasted!

If there's one kitchen appliance I can't live without, it's my Instant Pot. This gadget has changed my life completely in the kitchen! Gone are the days when I spent hours each week, prepping and then cooking meals. Often times those meals were tasteless, with leftovers that no one wanted to eat the next day.

Then along came my Instant Pot Pressure Cooker... this miraculous gift from the heavens helpls me make delectable meals every day. Quick cooking, tasty recipes - and I have leftovers my family fights over! From juicy pork shoulders to spicy rice dishes, you'll find a collection of mouthwatering and flavorsome Meditteranean recipes from every part of the world in this helpful and easy-to-read guide.

One of the most appealing features of the Instant Pot is that it makes fresh and fast homemade meals in no time.

Whether you're vegetarian or a lover of succulent barbecue meats, this book has the best recipes for making amazing, healthy meals. Don't forget to build in a couple cheat days to really test what your Instant Pot can do, because the possibilities are truly endless.

I want to share my favorite recipes with you, and I'll help you get familiar with the Instant Pot, so you know exactly how to use one. It'll change your life!

Introduction

The Mediterranean diet is more than a diet. It is a lifestyle. It's a way of eating in order to live a full and healthy life. When following this way of eating you'll not only lose weight, but you'll also strengthen your heart and provide your body with all the proper nutrients necessary to live a long and productive life. People following the Mediterranean diet have been linked to a lower risk of Alzheimer's disease and cancer, better overall cardiovascular health, and an extended lifespan. The building blocks that comprise a Mediterranean diet are foods rich in healthy oils, low in saturated fat, and filled with vegetables and fresh fruits. The Mediterranean diet focuses on typical foods and recipes you'd find in Mediterranean-style cooking. Here's what goes into the Mediterranean diet. This diet includes consuming lots of vegetables and grains, fruits, rice, and pasta while limiting fats, replacing salt with herbs and spices, and eating fish and poultry instead of red meat. The Mediterranean diet does not contain a lot of red meat. Nuts are a part of a healthy part of this diet. However, one should limit themselves to a handful or so a day.

Nuts have a high amount of fat, but a high percentage of the fat isn't saturated.

Nuts are also high in calories so carefully monitor the amount you eat. You'll want to avoid salted nuts and honey roasted or candied nuts.

It may ven include a glass of red wine per day, and regular physical activities to fully maximize the remarkable health benefits.

The Mediterranean diet reflects various eating habits of the countries near the Mediterranean Sea, mainly Southern Italy, Greece, Morocco, France, and Spain. Due to their unique locality, the climate supports fresh fruits, vegetables, and some of the world's best seafood.

This diet isn't focused on limiting your total consumption of fat, instead, it focuses on making smarter choices about the kinds of fat you consume. This diet discourages people from eating trans-fats and saturated fats, both of which have been linked to heart disease.

Grains used in the Mediterranean diet are preferably whole grain, which generally contains very little in the way of unhealthy trans-fat. Bread is an important part of the Mediterranean lifestyle; however, bread should not be covered in margarine or butter. Instead, the bread is eaten either dipped in olive oil or eaten plain.

This cuts down significantly on a number of trans and saturated fats normally associated with eating bread.

Wine plays a large role in the Mediterranean diet. A glass of wine is normally included with each evening meal.

This means 5 ounces or less of wine for anyone over the age of 65 and for people under 65 no more than 10 ounces daily. If you have any history of alcohol dependency or abuse, I suggest refraining altogether from consuming alcohol as part of your diet. The same goes if you already have liver or heart disease.

Olive oil is the primary source of fat in this type of diet. It actually provides monounsaturated fat, which is the kind of fat that helps reduce the levels of LDL cholesterol when utilized instead of trans or saturated fats.

The "Extra virgin" and "virgin" olive oils are considered to have undergone the least processing. They also happen to contain the largest levels of protective plant compounds responsible for providing antioxidant effects.

What is LDL?

Cholesterol is a compound belonging to the sterol or steroid alcohol subgroup of organic molecules. It is classified as a waxy steroid of fat.

It is an essential component of cellular membranes and a precursor to the production of fat-soluble vitamins, such as vitamin D.

There are two main types of cholesterol; HDL (high-density lipoproteins) and LDL (low-density lipoproteins). Though this is not entirely accurate. HDL and LDL are lipoproteins. They are the transport mechanisms for cholesterol particles. They are composed of proteins and fats.

LDL particles transport cholesterols from the liver to the cells of the body.

HDLs collect any that are found in the tissues or produced by other organs and carry it back to the liver for reprocessing.

This is why HDLs are sometimes referred to as "good" cholesterol because they pick up any that are dropped in the bloodstream before it can adhere to the walls of the arteries. LDL is known as bad cholesterol.

Although it is essential for life, large amounts of cholesterol in the bloodstream may increase a person's risk of heart disease, mainly atherosclerosis. This is why balance in HDL/LDL particles is so important, and an imbalance can be dangerous.

Highlight on Trans-fats

Trans-fats are listed as hydrogenated or partially hydrogenated oils. The oils may be soy, canola or simply listed as partially hydrogenated "vegetable" il. This kind of fat is the worst kind you can possibly eat.

According to the Mayo Clinic, trans-fats raise LDL levels and lowers HDL levels. It is a man-made fat that is found in baked goods and other packaged foods. In addition to causing HDL/LDL imbalance, it raises total blood triglycerides (fats that normally circulate in the bloodstream) and promotes plaque buildup on arterial walls. Like obesity, trans-fat also contributes to chronic inflammation.

Another major component of the Mediterranean diet is fatty fish. This includes lake trout, salmon, sardines, herring, mackerel, and albacore tuna. They have plenty of omega-3 fatty acids.

This type of fatty acid helps to decrease blood clotting and lower our triglyceride levels. High triglyceride levels (more than 150 mg/dL) can cause heart diseases. Omega-3 fatty acids are also associated with helping to moderate blood pressure, decrease the risk of sudden heart attack, and improve the overall health of our blood vessels.

I often get asked how many times per week can eat certain types of foods. Well, on the Mediterranean diet you can enjoy foods like yogurt, cheese, vegetables, whole grains, beans, and fruits daily. However, fish, eggs, and meat should only be served once or twice each week. You'll find that this is easier to do than you tink, especially after a couple of weeks once you've readjusted to your new way of eating. I have a ton of delicious recipes you can try out in later chapters.

The Mediterranean diet is 35 to 40 percent fat. However, the diet is focused primarily on healthy fats. Though higher in calories, fats make your food taste better and your meals feel more satisfying. You will eat a little less but enjoy your food significantly more.

I often hear people ask if they'll always feel hungry when following this diet. The answer to that is a resounding "NO."

Since the Mediterranean diet places emphasis on high fiber nutrients rich foods like vegetables, beans, fresh fruits, legumes, and whole grains you'll never have the intense hunger pangs associated with so many other diets on the market. You may be eating less each day, but your stomach won't feel that way.

The Mediterranean lifestyle itself plays a large role in supporting your diet plan. You'll want to get plenty of exercises but still carve out time to have long leisurely meals with your family and friends.

The good thing about the Mediterranean diet is that it doesn't require you to buy any special kind of foods. No money will be wasted on buying foods that are labeled as being low-fat or diet. Though there are exceptions, a Mediterranean diet consists of less processed, natural food. The more natural foods you incorporate into your daily diet, the healthier you'll be.

Being on a Mediterranean diet requires commitment. You'll be spending more time preparing your meals in your kitchen. Since you're eating natural foods, they won't already be processed and ready to go. I suggest brushing up on your cooking skills or taking a class if you have no skills to speak of. I love to cook so this wasn't too big of a change for me. However, I have friends who had zero skills in the kitchen, and they found this to be a daunting challenge at first. I plan out my weekly meals on Friday nights. Each Saturday I shop for all my food and then I prepare the majority of my meals in advance on Sunday.

Having a schedule and system in place makes the entire process go much smoother. It also ensures I always have a healthy meal on hand in case I'm feeling unmotivated to cook for myself at certain times of the week.

As with most diets, it's also very important to stay well hydrated when on this diet. Drink 64 oz. or 8 glasses of water on a daily basis. If you ever feel like you're getting a headache or a muscle cramp, you may just need some water.

I also suggest keeping a daily log of your meals. I go over what I use in the resources section. Keeping track of what you're eating is a good tool to help keep you motivated and on point. It will be a good way to identify the things throw you off course. For instance, when I first started, I noticed my food intake was terrible on Sunday.

This was because for much of the year I would spend Sunday afternoons watching football with friends while eating and drinking non-stop. Once I saw what I was consuming compared to the rest of my week, I knew what changes I needed to make to keep me on track.

Don't forget to check with your physician before starting on this diet.

I know it sounds like a giant hassle, but you should always determine a proper course of action with a trained professional before getting started.

Major Features of a Mediterranean Diet:
1. The primary source of your fat in this diet is olive oil.
2. Dinner often includes a glass of red wine.
3. Vegetables and seasonal fresh fruits are a major part of every meal.
4. Whole grain pasta and bread are served without any type of apology,
5. Meat is consumed in smaller portions, and red meat is primarily avoided altogether.
6. Popular flavors include garlic, basil, oregano, lemon, rosemary, and mint.

Benefits of the Mediterranean Diet

Many studies prove the many advantages of the Mediterranean Diet. However, even if you don't look at the studies, the Mediterranean people serve as first-hand proof of the benefits of this wonderful diet. Here are a number of benefits from going on the Mediterranean Diet.

Long and Healthy Life

The Mediterranean cuisine is often referred to as the healthiest cuisine in the world, and the diet doesn't stray too far away. Being based mostly on fresh vegetables and fruits, healthy oils and whole grains, as well as lean meat and seafood, it's not hard to see why this diet is considered to be healthy. Mix with a glass of red wine, and you've got yourself a fun, easy going diet.

Your Heart Will Thank You

Scientific evidence easily connects good heart health with certain foods, mainly vegetables, fruits, olive oil, and nuts. The Mediterranean diet has it all!

The Mediterranean diet is all about highlighting healthy fats.

Instead of using the usual cooking oil, the diet uses olive oil which contains healthy fat that is good for the heart. With that said, the Mediterranean Diet can help decrease your risk of heart failure.

A Mediterranean diet consists of food with monounsaturated fats like olive oil rather than saturated fats like butter.

The Mediterranean diet naturally includes most of the key diet changes that would keep your heart in tip-top shape

Shed Some Unwanted Weight

Although the main focus of this diet is not weight loss, it will surely help with it if that's what you're looking for. Just look at it from this point of view: fresh, clean food combined with whole grains, good fats, less sugar and plenty of liquids coupled with copious amounts of exercise. By transitioning to healthy foods and a healthy lifestyle, you'll shed pounds without causing drastic imbalances in your body. Also, it is known that plant-based diets like the Mediterranean diet are really helpful in losing weight. The mere fact that you stopped eating junk food and processed food with sugar and unhealthy fats is already a very good start to weight loss!

Controls Diabetes

Because it focuses on fresh ingredients and it packs plenty of vitamins, antioxidants, and minerals, this diet is a great way to keep your diabetes under control. This lifestyle controls excess insulin, which in turn lowers our blood sugar levels.

Regulating blood sugar levels is vastly important to living a healthier lifestyle.

There is a need for balancing a lot of whole foods into this plan to find quality sources of protein and consume carbs that are low in sugar. That makes the body burn fat much more efficiently, and you will have more energy as a result.

In short, a natural diet with fresh produce is a natural combater of diabetes.

It is Affordable

The Mediterranean diet is accessible even if you're on a budget. Legumes, vegetables, fruits, herbs, whole grains, and olive oil are not as expensive as they sound, but they offer so much versatility in the kitchen.

Boost Brain Power

The Mediterranean Diet can also countcract the brain's poor ability to perform.

Choosing this lifestyle will actually help you preserve your memory, leading to an overall increase in your cognitive health.

Normally cognitive disorders are caused by a scenario where your brain is unable to get sufficient amount of dopamine.

Dopamine is a compound or chemical present in the brain responsible for passing information from one neuron to the other. It is responsible for thought processing, mood regulation, and proper body movements.

The ability of the Mediterranean diet to help boost your cognitive health is normally linked to the combination of its anti-inflammatory fruits and vegetables, its healthy fats and nuts.

These foods normally battle cognitive decline that is caused by age. But how do these foods do it?

These foods normally deal with elements that cause impaired brain function like inflammation, free radicals, and exposure to toxicity.

Fatty fish, nuts and olive oils all contain omega 3 fatty acids that usually help reduce the level of inflammation in your body. Such vegetables like spinach, kale, and broccoli that are dark green contain vitamin E, which is known to protect your body from an anti-inflammatory molecule known as cytokines.

Vegetables like spinach, broccoli, and fruits like raspberries, cherries, and watermelon all have antioxidants that neutralize free radicals that affect your brain. The Mediterranean diet also tends to focus on monounsaturated fats which come from oils like olive oil. The oils and the fatty acids that you get from omega 3 (from fish) combine to keep your arteries unblocked.

That automatically increases the health of your brain and reduces your risk of getting diseases like Alzheimer disease and dementia.

Encourage Relaxation

The Mediterranean Diet surprisingly enough can encourage relaxation. The diet can lower your levels of insulin and make you feel at ease. High blood sugar can cause you to be hyperactive and later crash; but eating balanced meals with lots of whole grains, fruits, veggies, etc. actually helps stabilize blood sugar, allowing you to relax and rest. Since a major component of this lifestyle is eating with the family at the dinner table, relaxation is maximized. With a home-cooked meal in your comfort zone, relaxation will be evident with this dict.

Enhance Your Mood

The diet can help you to be positive, even when things aren't going your way.

Healthy living does that. When you have eaten enough food to fuel you with lots of nutrients, your body notices. Fulfillment and productivity enhance your mood. For one, applying the diet correctly will make you feel like you're doing something good for yourself, and thus enhances your overall mood.

Improve Skin Condition

Fish have Omega-3 fatty acids. They strengthen the skin membrane and make it more elastic and firmer. Olive oil, red wine, and tomatoes contain a lot of antioxidants to protect against skin damage brought about by chemical reactions and prolonged sun exposure.

Disadvantages of the Mediterranean Diet

While the Mediterranean Diet clearly has incredible benefits and has proven to be really effective in keeping terminal illnesses at bay for generations, it's worth noting that it also has some disadvantages. After all, a perfect diet does not exist.

1. **Not Specific.** The Mediterranean works its magic and all, but it's the spell you need to know to make it work. However, the diet really does not have a specific "spell." For instance, the foods in the diet vary as the different Mediterranean countries and cities use different varieties of it. For example, Greece and Italy have different preferred food on their tables. There are no official and exact names of certain foods to eat; it only shows generic terminology like fruits, vegetables, fish, and more. Additionally, it doesn't show how much to eat so it could get quite tricky to know exactly if you've overeaten or if you did not follow the diet at all.

2. **Not for some people**. Some of the foods included in the diet have gluten, and there are people who are sensitive to gluten. People with peanut and seafood allergies would also find it hard to follow the Mediterranean Diet as nuts and fish are a major part of the diet. Also, as the diet could require planning the menu and preparing the dishes at home, those who don't have time to cook will find it challenging to follow this.

3. **Not an overnighter**. The Mediterranean people are as healthy as they are because their diet is traditional; they have been on it their whole lives. So if you expect results after one day, reign in those unrealistic expectations. In order to get positive, long-lasting results, don't let the Mediterranean Diet be just a passing diet craze. You have to breathe it, live it, and eat it; just like real Mediterranean people.

Being Keen on a Mediterranean Diet

If you don't manage your diet closely, you may suffer from these common side effect. Luckily, there are easy ways to prevent these from becoming an issue.

1. You may start to gain weight if you don't monitor the amount of nuts and olive oil you consume. These are very high in fat, so you need to keep an eye on how much you're having each day.
2. You could have some calcium loss from eating less dairy. If it happens to you, ask your doctor if you should begin taking some form of calcium supplement.
3. You may find that your iron levels are low. Be sure to eat more foods rich in vitamin C or iron.

If you have any issues with alcohol, I suggest abstaining from incorporating it into your diet. The idea is to get healthy not endanger yourself further.

As you can tell the side effects are pretty minimal in relation to most other diets.

Not only that but these side effects are easily reversed with a little bit of attention on your part.

*For the first few weeks of your diet your body will be adjusting and purging itself of all the built up toxins in your body. During this time frame, you may feel ill or unwell at times. This is completely normal.

Once your body has rid itself of all the excess toxins and sugars in your body, you'll notice an increase in energy and noticeable improvement in your overall well-being.

Five Rules for Rapid Weight Loss

For the success of the Mediterranean Diet, you need to adhere to the following rules:

Rule #1: Ensure That You Focus On Plant-Based Foods

When preparing your meals, ensure that you that the seasonal fresh ingredients that include vegetables, fruits, whole grains, legumes, and nuts.

Rule #2: Adapt to Using Healthy Oil

When on a Mediterranean Diet, fats are very important. But ensure you are ingesting the correct ones by using natural oils instead of butter.

Rule #3: Get Good Protein Selections

Do not consume red meat or beef on a daily basis. Instead, you can enjoy once a week. Get used to alternative sources like poultry, fish, eggs, or cheese.

Rule #4: Go Local and Ensure Your Ingredients are Fresh

In the Mediterranean, nations experience different seasons. Most foods are grown locally and will always be fresh from the market or store.

It ensures that your meals are prepared with the available ingredients depending on the season making them fresh and healthy.

Rule #5: Eat Smaller Amounts

To enjoy the rich, delicious, and healthy Mediterranean foods, control your intake. Eat small bites to ensure that you taste more food, ingest less and enjoy all the health benefits.

Top Hints for Your Success

If you are interested in applying the Mediterranean diet to your life to lose weight, then these general dieting tips paired with the Mediterranean diet eating habits will help you maximize your weight loss.

Eat Slowly

It takes twenty minutes for your food to start digesting and give you a feeling of fullness after you eat a meal. Therefore, slow down and chew your food so that you can actually taste it and enjoy the flavor.

If you tend to eat fast, you may find that you eat more because it takes that twenty minutes to get your internal system fired up.

Drink Water Before Your Meal

Try drinking a full eight-ounce glass of water before you sit down to eat a meal.

Sometimes thirst can be mistaken for a feeling of hunger. Drinking a glass of water before you eat can get the digestion process started quicker which can cause you to eat less during a meal.

Split Your Plate Into Three Sections

Visually split your plate in half then split one of those halves in two. This makes three sections.... two small ones and one big one.

The big section is for vegetables, and the two smaller sections are for your starches and proteins.

You can use this as a measuring guide when you go out to eat or want to transition your dinner plate into healthier portions. You will receive the highest levels of phytonutrients from vegetables, so that is why vegetables occupy the largest section of the plate.

Exercise

Adhere to the lowest, most foundational level of the Mediterranean pyramid which is a daily activity. Do your best to get thirty minutes of exercise every day.

Change the Way You Think About Food

See vegetables and fruits as snacks. Slice your vegetables into ready to eat snack sizes and wash your fruits when you bring them home from the store so that they are ready to grab as a quick snack when you're feeling hungry.

Always have a jar of mixed nuts within your reach in the kitchen counter and eat a handful of those along with your vegetable or fruit snack.

Replace butter and margarine with olive oil. I especially like to use olive oil when grilling sandwiches or toasting my breads where at one time I only used butter or margarine.

Prepackage Snacks

Prepackage snacks into portion sizes rather than eating from the full container. This can prevent overeating.

When you pre-allocate how much of a snack you're going to eat, then you're helping yourself stay disciplined.

Snack Two or Three Times a Day

Enjoy two or three snacking times a day where you eat a serving of fruit or vegetables with no salt or sugar added. Schedule a snack in the morning, afternoon, and before bed.

Replace Cakes and Cookies

Replace frequent cake and cookie binges with a serving of popcorn cooked in olive oil and sprinkled with parmesan cheese or garlic powder rather than salt and butter.

Buy Smaller Plates and Bowls

When you fill up a smaller plate or bowl, you can still get the satisfaction of having a full plate or bowl.

With a smaller bowl/plate, you can feel satisfied but still be able to eat in healthy portions that adhere to the Mediterranean diet food pyramid.

Replace Saturated Fats with Monounsaturated Fats

Give your weight loss program the super-charged fuel it needs by replacing your saturated fats with monounsaturated fats. The Mediterranean diet replaces a standard bad fat diet with high levels of healthy monounsaturated fats that raise good cholesterol levels.

Learn a Well-Balanced Eating Plan

The longer you adhere to the Mediterranean diet the more energy and vitality you will receive.

The Mediterranean diet offers a well-balanced eating plan that includes the correct amount of each food group.

Is The Mediterranean Diet Healthy?

Here is a secret for you. Most popular healthy diets that are touted for weight loss—from Paleo to Whole 30 to Clean Eating to Mediterranean and Vegetarian—share the same principles.

They involve consuming whole foods (contrary to packaged and processed) and bringing in some quality protein, healthy fats, complex carbs, fiber and mineral-rich veggies to your plate. However, each of these diets presents you a marginally different path that leads to fulfilling these principles.

That's why I'll be breaking them down for you so you can figure out which one (if any!) is right for you. I'll also quickly explain the facts and provide you with quick and actionable tips on how to follow the Mediterranean diet as part of a healthy and nutritious life.

A Brief History of the Mediterranean Diet
Mediterranean cuisine refers to the style of food commonly enjoyed in the countries surrounding the Mediterranean Sea, such as Spain, Italy, and Greece among others.

There are around 22 countries situated in the Mediterranean basin, notably: Italy, Greece and Southern France, all bringing a wide cultural diversity to the menu. There are also foods from Eastern Europe, and the added touches from the Eastern shores of the African continent. There is no single diet, as it is an accumulation of regional variances. This lends an eclectic variety of ingredients, and various ways of cooking them. The influence of the Mediterranean diet began to spread throughout the world in the 1950's. The hot climate has a major influence on the diet. With little rainfall, there is little grazing for cattle. That is the reason the indigenous people of these lands turn to what they can cultivate. The sun provides them with an abundance of rich fruits and various vegetables. Seafood also plays a major role in meals on the coastlines of the Mediterranean Sea. Hardy animals that are able to survive dry conditions, such as goats and chickens add to the cuisine as well.

The Science behind the Mediterranean Diet

The ever-growing problem of cardiovascular discase has been a major concern with regards to the modern Western diet, which was adopted by a significant chunk of the world's population during the 20th century.

In the 1970's, the diet was compared to the Western dietary intake of high carb and sugary foods. This led scientists to wonder why those living in the Mediterranean regions have such low rates of this deadly condition. The main study in the 1980's was known as the MONICA (Multinational Monitoring of Trends and Determinants in Cardiovascular Disease). It collated over 10 years' worth of data, and included twenty-one countries. The results were so pivotal, that they are the foundation of the belief that this is the best diet on the planet. Another study in 2003, took 772 participants, and the tests lasted three months[1]. Again, the results showed a larger DECREASE in blood sugar and blood pressure levels, for those on the Mediterranean style diet, than for those on a low-fat diet[2]. In other studies, the increased consumption of nuts (over a five year period) has shown a 16-63% REDUCED risk of cardiovascular death[3]. The lower mortality rates of those who cook daily with olive oil, is just one of the many excellent reasons to change to the Mediterranean way of eating.

---

[1] https://academic.oup.com/advances/article/5/3/330S/4562746
[2] https://www.ncbi.nlm.nih.gov/pubmed/16818923
[3] https://www.healthline.com/nutrition/5-studies-on-the-mediterranean-diet#section2

Super Health Benefits of a Mediterranean Diet

With the findings of a 30% reduction in heart disease, published in 2013 from a study by the New England Journal of Medicine called PREDIMED, we should take these constant studies seriously[4]. Mediterranean diet reduces cardiovascular risk. Isn't that inviting enough to encourage you to change your diet? How about the studies that proved Mediterranean foods stop the brain shrinking with age, which had been correlated to the high intake of plant-based foods?

The food on the tables of the families living in the Mediterranean area are without a doubt more wholesome and nutritious than the typical Western diet. The ingredients include fish (at least twice a week), providing high protein along with omega 3 fat. Whilst on the topic of fats, the olive oil they use comes from the olives they personally cultivate. Olive oil contains lots of monounsaturated fatty acids. These are good fats with many benefits. One is that it helps reduce the risk of heart disease and strokes.

---

[4] https://www.nejm.org/doi/full/10.1056/NEJMoa1200303

Other foods are outsized portions of vegetables and fruit, nuts, seeds, legumes and basically any whole grains.

What you will NOT find on their tables are the high in saturated fats, sugars, and salt-processed foods. These foods contribute to the development of cardiovascular disease in the Western diet.

If you can maintain a healthy Mediterranean Diet, the number of health benefits are endless.

• Eating healthier can lead to a longer life. Not only does it increase your lifespan, but also makes you feel healthier and fitter for longer, well into your golden age.

• This is not a restrictive diet. With our recipes, you will learn that you are eliminating certain types of food from your diet. Yet with so loose and easy to follow guidelines, you can enjoy cooking and eating again.

• A Mediterranean style diet is not expensive. After all, it's up to you how much to spend on food and where to buy it. It's pricier to order take out or to frequent pricy restaurants, so try to limit them.

• You can also go vegetarian and bulk up your meals with legumes, as opposed to having meats. They not only provide ample protein, but also a great amount of fiber.

• As we have said before, and will continue to reiterate, the secret is in the oil. ALWAYS use olive oil. Buy the best you can and if you can afford it, get the EVOO. If you need oil that gets hot without smoking, use light olive oil. Your heart will be grateful for the rest of your life.

The Changes Happening When You Are on a Mediterranean Diet

Not only will your heart thank you for embracing a Mediterranean-style diet, there are other positive changes that will occur in your body like:

• Lower blood sugar levels. Ideal for Diabetes Type II.

• Stronger muscles and bones. Studies have shown a 70% increase in strength for the elderly on a Mediterranean Diet[5].

• Eating healthy antioxidants reduces the effects of brain shrinkage in old age. The move reduces the risk of neuro-degeneration diseases, such as Parkinson's and Alzheimer's.

• Reduce the risk of cancerous cells developing.

• Increase energy and better concentrations skills.

• Reduce chances of neurological diseases.

• Helps fight inflammations.

---

[5] https://www.ncbi.nlm.nih.gov/pmc/articles/PMC2544374/

• Produce higher rates of dopamine in the brain, leading to a feeling of well-being and improved mood.

• All that vitamin E will improve skin condition and make it glow.

• Lose weight, so long as you monitor portion sizes and exercise regularly.

How to Lose Weight Fast When in Mediterranean Diet

When you think of pizzas and pastas, you do not associate these foods with weight loss. While you can still eat carbs on this diet, you should not eat large portions of them. Pasta tends to be a side dish, about a half of a cup, set on a great plate of vegetables and salad.

• The focus on how Mediterranean people eat, is not just about the food; it includes such things as smaller portions and exercising. Their pace of life also seems to be less demanding.

• Feel fuller for longer, as you will be eating more protein-based ingredients. This will deter you from eating snacks between meals. However, some relevant snack recipes are included.

• The ingredients of the Mediterranean style diet naturally tend to be low in calories and high in fiber.

This is the perfect combination to get rid of excess fat reserves.

• Go for the low-fat options such as Greek yogurt, milk, and cheese when choosing dairy products.

• Red meat should be consumed only a couple of times a month, if at all. White meats are fine, so long they are the lean options.

• The secret of this way of eating is the olive oil. Use nothing else but extra virgin olive oil (EVOO) and you too will live a long and healthier life.

What is an Instant Pot Pressure Cooker?

So now, let's learn all about the Instant Pot so you can start cooking!

Now that you know how much I love my Instant Pot, you'll want to know just what an electric pressure cooker is. The Instant Pot is an appliance that's a combination of a pressure cooker, slow cooker, rice cooker, and yogurt maker – all in one handy kitchen device.

What parts make up the Instant Cooker? There's an outer pot, which is the base and heat source for the pressure cooker. Inside of this outer pot goes the inner pot, which is made from durable stainless steel. This inner pot is where all the cooking happens.

There's a lid that goes on top of the inner pot, with a silicone ring that seals tightly to keep food, liquids, and pressure securely in the pot.

On top of the lid are the pressure release and the float valve. The pressure release does just that – it releases pressure from inside the Instant Pot. The float valve on the lid pops up when the Instant Pot is pressurized and lowers back down when it's not. It becomes safe to open the lid of the inner pot when the float valve is down.

The Instant Pot has a condensation collector on the side of the base unit that can be removed. Its purpose is to collect condensation, usually when the Instant Pot is being used as a slow cooker.

With regard to the Instant Pot's model you possess, it may come with some useful accessories – a steaming rack, measuring cup, and a set of spoons.Not a complex appliance at all, right?

Get to know your brand of Instant Pot by taking a few minutes to read the instruction manual. Even though all electric pressure cookers have pretty much the same functions and settings, every brand comes with some unique features.

How to USE the Instant Pot

When you first get your Instant Pot don't be intimidated by all the buttons, functions, andprograms.

That's what my recipe book is for – to guide you through the steps of using an electric pressure cooker with little confusion. Here are some basic things to know about your Instant Pot that can make it easy for you to start cooking.

Just what is pressure cooking?

Let's get some of the technical information out of the way so you can get to the good stuff... the recipes! The Instant Pot uses a cooking method that seals ingredients and liquids inside a sealed pot. It uses heat to create steam, which then builds up the pressure in the pot. This steam is released or trapped in the pot to control the amount of pressure. With a presence of more pressure, the temperatures will also be higher– and the food cooks faster. Sound complex? Your Instant Pot cooks food fast, fast, fast!

Foods to Eat?

Replacing saturated and hydrogenated fats with olive oil is one of the major differences you'll notice about the Mediterranean diet. Everything is cooked in olive oil. That includes salad dressings and marinades. Of course, they grow their own olives in the Mediterranean regions, so it's no surprise this oil is so popular. Other healthy choices are options too, like avocados which are great for oil.

Primarily, you are increasing your plant-based foods. Don't cook with butter when a recipe asks to use olive oil. Don't use sugar to make foods tasty, use herbs and spices instead. Red meat does not have to be off the menu (prepare only a couple of times every month), but white lean meat is better. Fish is also an important ingredient in this diet, and should be served at least twice a week.

In this section, major foodstuffs will be outlined. Think of it as a pyramid, with the top ingredients of the list making the large foundation. As you go down the list, the pyramid gets smaller, so eat less of these ingredients:

1. The foundation of the pyramid consists of being substantial and social. Having family meals, dancing with friends, walking, and sports. These are all activities that people who live in hot climates always take part of, but all of it plays a role in the Mediterranean way of life.
2. All vegetables, including tubers and root vegetables.
3. Fruits- dates, grapes, melons, strawberries, bananas, kiwis.
4. Legumes- including peas, lentils, peanuts, chickpeas and other types of beans.

5. Whole grains- such as oats, rice (wild or brown are better), rye, barley, buckwheat, corn, pasta (whole wheat better), whole-wheat bread (not buttered).
6. Nuts- for example hazelnut, cashew, walnut, almond (but only a handful daily).
7. Seeds- like the sunflower and pumpkin.
8. Herbs and spices like garlic, basil, nutmeg and cinnamon.
9. Seafood and oily fish, from salmon to sardines, or lobster, shrimp and oysters.
10. Poultry like chicken and duck.
11. Dairy such as Greek yogurt, cheese and milk.
12. Eggs.
13. Red wine (no more than 5oz daily - if you miss a day, no doing a double). If you don't like alcohol, then drink purple grape juice.

What Foods to Avoid

When learning any new diet, it's also important to learn which foods should NOT be included. Another important factor is to read the labels on everything. It is the only way to be completely aware of what goes into the food you eat.

Here's a quick note for inspiration:

- Foods considered to be processed, such as sausages and bread should be eaten in moderation. DON'T have any that are super processed, such as hotdogs, take outs, pastries. They are exceptionally high in sugars and salt, Ingredients and proven to be linked to cancer risks.
- Check the sugar levels if they are labeled as "low fat"
- DO NOT add sugar to tea and coffee.
- ALWAYS check that sugar content is not high on the ingredients list. The higher it is on the list, the more there is in the food contents. Many readymade foods such as sauces, milk and even bread have it.
- AVOID foods made with refined grains. That means that the process has removed all the important dietary fiber, such as white bread, white flour, white rice, and white pasta.
- AVOID bad fats and refined oils. Anything labeled with *trans fats* or *hydrogenated fats* is bad for you. These can be in foods such as margarines, cakes, even microwave popcorn. Don't use oils such as canola, soy, soybean etc. outlearn about the types of fats used in the food you eat, whenever you can.

- DO NOT buy if "trans fats" is listed anywhere on the label.
- Take out will not have labels, but they use lots of trans fats for cooking. In fact, most resturants overcompensate with obscene amounts of sugar and butter to make food tastier, so as a general rule of thumb, resturants are not healthy places to eat. BEWARE of them!

Breakfast Recipes

Cottage Cheese soufflé

Servings: 5

Ingredients:

- 9 oz. cottage cheese
- 3 tbsps. raisins
- 1 tsp. vanilla sugar
- 3 tbsps. brown sugar
- 3 egg yolks
- 4 peaches
- 5 tbsps. sour cream
- ½ c. cream

Directions:

1. Chop the raisins carefully.
2. Combine the vanilla sugar with the brown sugar.
3. Add cottage cheese and egg yolks.
4. Place the mixture in the blender and blend it well.
5. Chop the peaches and add them to the blender too.
6. Pour the cream and sour cream in the blender and start to blend it for 30 seconds more.
7. Then transfer the soufflé mixture in the ramekins and put the ramekins in the instant pot.
8. Close the lid and cook the dish at the pressure mode for 5 minutes.
9. Then chill the cottage cheese soufflé for a little time.
10. Serve it!

Nutritional Information:

calories 219, fat 10.1g, carbs 26.9g, protein 7g

Milky breakfast couscous

Servings: 3

Ingredients:

- 2 c. couscous
- 2 c. milk
- 1 tbsp. butter
- 1 tsp. vanilla sugar
- ¼ tsp. ground cardamom
- 1 tbsp. sugar

Directions:

1. Combine the couscous with the milk in the instant pot.
2. Add butter and vanilla sugar.
3. After this, add ground cardamom and sugar.
4. Stir the liquid mixture well with the help of the wooden spatula.
5. Close the lid and cook the dish at the porridge mode for 15 minutes.
6. When the couscous is cooked – put it in the serving bowls immediately.
7. Enjoy!

Nutritional Information:

Calories: 279, Fat:10.2g, Carbs:37.19g, Protein: 9g

Mediterranean egg cake

Servings: 5

Ingredients:

- 1 c. cherry tomatoes
- 1 white onion
- 1 tsp. salt
- ½ tsp. ground black pepper
- 8 eggs
- ½ c. cream
- 1 c. parsley
- 1 tsp. oregano
- 3 tbsps. chives
- 2 tbsps. butter

Directions:

1. Peel the onion and slice it.
2. Cut the cherry tomatoes into the halves.
3. Beat the eggs in the instant pot and whisk them gently.
4. Then add the cherry tomato halves and sliced onion.
5. Sprinkle the mixture with the ground black pepper and salt.
6. Chop the parsley and add it in the instant pot too.
7. Then add butter and chives.
8. In the end, add the oregano and do not stir the mixture at all.
9. Close the lid and cook the egg cake at the pressure mode for 15 minutes.
10. When the egg cake is cooked – remove it from the instant pot and cut into the pieces.
11. Serve it!

Nutritional Information:

Calories:312, Fat:24.8g, Carbs:6.22g, Protein: 16g

Almond quinoa

Servings: 4

Ingredients:

- ½ c. almonds
- ½ c. cream
- ½ c. water
- 1 c. milk
- 1 tsp. vanilla extract
- ¼ tsp. ground nutmeg
- 2 c. quinoa
- ½ c. strawberry

Directions:

1. Combine the cream and water in the instant pot.
2. Crush the almond well and add them in the instant pot.
3. Add vanilla extract and ground nutmeg.
4. Blend the strawberries and them in the instant pot too.
5. Then add the quinoa and mix up the mixture well with the help of the spoon.
6. When you get the homogenous texture of the quinoa – close the instant pot lid.
7. Adjust the instant pot to 15 minutes and cook the dish.
8. When the time is over and the quinoa absorbs all the liquid – it is done.
9. Serve it hot.
10. Add the liquid honey is desired.
11. Enjoy!

Nutritional Information:

calories 419, fat 13.1g, carbs 60.1g, protein 15g

Main dishes

Pasta frittata

Servings: 7

Ingredients:

- 6 oz. cooked pasta
- ½ c. cream
- 5 eggs
- ½ c. tomatoes
- 1 tsp. olive oil
- ½ c. spinach
- 1 tsp. salt
- 1 tsp. butter
- 1 tbsp. almond flour
- 1 tsp. ground white pepper
- 2 tsps. dried oregano
- 1 tsp. dill
- 1 sweet red pepper

Directions:

1. Beat the eggs in the blender and blend them well.
2. Chop the tomatoes.
3. Add the cream in the blended egg mixture.
4. Then chop the spinach and add it to the egg mixture too.
5. Sprinkle the mixture with the salt, butter, and almond flour.
6. After this, add ground white pepper, dill, and dried oregano,
7. Chop the sweet pepper and add it to the egg mixture.
8. Blend the mass at the medium speed for 30 seconds.
9. Spray the instant pot vessel with the olive oil inside.
10. Then put the pasta in the instant pot.
11. Chop the tomatoes and put them on the pasta.
12. Pour the blended egg mixture and stir it gently to not damage the pasta.
13. Close the instant pot lid and cook the dish at the pressure mode for 12 minutes.
14. When the time is over – the frittata is cooked.
15. Serve it hot.

16. Enjoy!

Nutritional Information:

calories 177, fat 11.8g, carbs 10.27g, protein 8g

Chicken juicy meatballs

Servings: 8

Ingredients:

- 3 c. ground chicken
- 2 tbsps. oregano
- 1 tsp. dried dill
- 1 tsp. parsley
- 1 tsp. salt
- 1 tbsp. onion powder
- 4 garlic cloves
- 1 tbsp. sesame seeds
- 1 egg
- 2 tsps. capers
- 1 c. bread crumbs
- 1 small potato
- ½ c. plain yogurt
- 2 tbsps. butter

Directions:

1. Slice the garlic cloves and combine them with the oregano, dried dill, and parsley.
2. Sprinkle the mixture with the salt and onion powder.
3. After this beat the egg in the bowl and whisk it.
4. Add the ground chicken and garlic clove mass.
5. Add capers and plain yogurt.
6. After this, peel the potato and grate it.
7. Add the grated potato in the ground chicken mixture.
8. Then add sesame seeds.
9. Stir it carefully and make the medium balls.
10. Toss the butter in the instant pot.
11. Then put the meatballs and close the lid.
12. Cook the dish at the poultry mode for 17 minutes.
13. When the meatballs are cooked – cool them little.
14. Serve the dish!

Nutritional Information:

calories 232, fat 12.2g, carbs 14.82g, protein 17g

Tomato shrimps

Servings: 5

Ingredients:

- ½ c. tomatoes
- 7 tbsps. tomato paste
- ¼ c. tomato juice
- 1 tbsp. sugar
- 1 tsp. salt
- 1 tsp. ground black pepper
- 1 tbsp. paprika
- 14 oz. shrimps
- ¼ c. garlic
- 1 white onion
- ¼ c. arugula
- 1 tsp. cilantro
- 1 tbsp. olive oil
- 4 tbsps. cream

Directions:

1. Combine the tomato paste and tomato juice together.
2. Add sugar and salt.
3. Then sprinkle the liquid with the ground black pepper and paprika.
4. Chop the garlic and arugula.
5. Add the ingredients in the tomato liquid.
6. Pour it in the instant pot and sauté it for 10 minutes.
7. Meanwhile, peel the onion and dice it.
8. Combine the diced onion with the cilantro, olive oil, and cream,
9. Then chop the tomatoes and add them to the onion mixture.
10. When the tomato liquid starts to boil – add the onion mixture and stir it well.
11. Peel the shrimps and add them in the instant pot.
12. Close the lid and cook the dish at the pressure mode for 7 minutes.
13. When the dish is done – transfer the shrimps in the serving plates.
14. Ladle the small amount of the tomato sauce from the instant pot.
15. Serve it hot.
16. Enjoy!

Nutritional Information:

calories 182, fat 6.5g, carbs 13.19g, protein 19g

Rosemary beef steak

Servings: 4

Ingredients:

- 3 tbsps. pomegranate sauce
- 1 lb. beef steak
- 1 tbsp. liquid honey
- ¼ c. fresh rosemary
- ¼ c. fresh dill
- 1 tbsp. balsamic vinegar
- ¼ lemon
- 1 tbsp. lemon zest
- 2 tbsps. olive oil
- 1 tsp. garlic powder
- 1 tsp. salt

Directions:

1. Beat the beef steak gently.
2. Sprinkle it with the fresh rosemary and fresh dill.
3. Mix up the meat carefully.
4. After this, sprinkle the beef steak with the liquid honey and balsamic vinegar.
5. Rub it with the lemon zest and garlic powder.
6. After this, sprinkle the meat with the salt.
7. Stir it carefully with the help of the fingertips.
8. Squeeze the lemon juice in the meat.
9. Spread the beef steak with the pomegranate sauce.
10. Then put the beef steak in the instant pot.
11. Close the lid and cook the meat at the pressure mode for 10 minutes.
12. Open the lid and turn the meat to the other side and cook it for 10 minutes more.
13. Then chill the cooked beef steak for at least 10 minutes.
14. Serve the meat only hot.
15. Enjoy!

Nutritional Information:

calories 252, fat 13.9g, carbs 7.34g, protein 24g

Curry squid

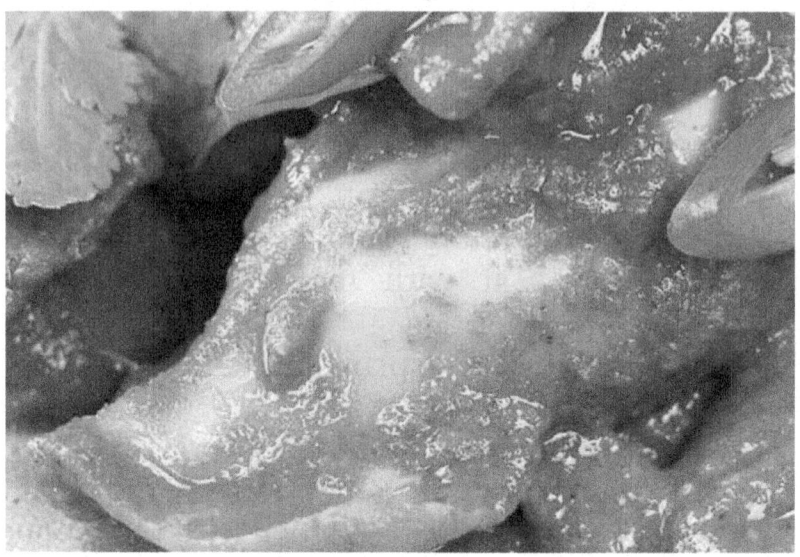

Servings: 6

Ingredients:

- 12 oz. squid
- 1 tbsp. curry paste
- ½ c. almond milk
- 1 tsp. salt
- 1 tsp. chili flakes
- 1 tsp. oregano
- 1 tsp. ground black pepper
- 1 tsp. cilantro
- 1 tsp. curry
- ¼ c. black olives
- 1 orange
- 2 tbsps. butter
- 1 tbsp. minced garlic
- 1 tsp. dried ginger
- 4 tbsps. fish sauce

Directions:

1. Wash the squid very carefully.
2. Combine the curry paste, almond milk, salt, chili flakes, oregano, ground black pepper, cilantro, curry, minced garlic, dried dill, and fish sauce.
3. Whisk the mixture.
4. Grate the orange to get the orange zest.
5. Then squeeze the orange juice into the curry paste mixture.
6. Add the orange zest.
7. Then spread the squid with the curry paste mixture and leave it for 20 minutes to marinate.
8. Put the marinated squid in the instant pot and close the lid.
9. Adjust the instant pot mode to 10 minutes.
10. When the time is over – serve the squid immediately.

Nutritional Information:

calories 118, fat 5.7g, carbs 6.75g, protein 10g

Side dishes

Warm Colorful salad

Servings: 7

Ingredients:

- 8 oz. beetroot
- 1 carrot
- 2 sweet red peppers
- 1 tbsp. sesame seeds
- ¼ c. black olives
- 1 c. arugula
- 1/3 c. fresh cilantro
- 1 tsp. salt
- 1 c. chicken stock
- 1 tsp. fish sauce
- 1 tsp. ground ginger
- ½ tsp. cayenne pepper
- 1 tbsp. olive oil
- 1 tsp. apple cider vinegar
- 3 peaches
- ¼ c. cream

Directions:

1. Peel the beetroot and chop it.
2. Peel the carrot and cut it into the small cubes.
3. Then chop the fresh cilantro and peaches.
4. Combine all the ingredients together in the big bowl.
5. Discard the seeds from the sweet red peppers and chop them into the same cubes as the carrot.
6. Add the peppers in the bowl too.
7. Sprinkle the mixture with the sesame seeds, fish sauce, chicken stock, cayenne pepper, apple cider vinegar, and cream.
8. Mix up the mixture carefully with the help of the plastic spatula.
9. After this, add salt.
10. Transfer the bowl mixture in the instant pot.
11. Close the lid and cook the vegetables at the pressure mode for 15 minutes.
12. When the vegetables start to be tender – remove them from the instant pot and transfer to the big bowl.
13. Sprinkle the mixture with the olive oil.
14. Chop the arugula and slice the black olives.
15. Add the ingredients in the mass and stir it.
16. Transfer the cooked warm salad in the serving plates.

17. Enjoy!

Nutritional Information:

calories 109, fat 5.5g, carbs 13.79g, protein 3g

Sweet corn mix

Servings: 6

Ingredients:

- 1 c. sweet corn
- ½ chili pepper
- 3 c. chicken stock
- 1 tsp. butter
- 1 tsp. olive oil
- 1 tsp. salt
- 1 c. quinoa
- 2 tbsps. sour cream
- 1 onion
- 1 c. sweet pepper
- 2 garlic cloves
- ¼ c. green peas
- 2 tbsps. canola oil
- 1 tbsp. oregano

Directions:

1. Chop the chili pepper into the tiny pieces.
2. Combine the chili pepper and sweet corn together.
3. Put the quinoa in the instant pot.
4. Add chicken stock and butter.
5. After this, add olive oil, salt, canola oil, and oregano.
6. Sprinkle the mixture with the sweet corn mass and stir it carefully with the wooden spatula.
7. Add sweet pepper.
8. Peel the onion and dice it.
9. Add the diced onion and sour cream in the instant pot.
10. Close the lid and cook the mixture at the sauté mode for 45 minutes
11. When the sweet corn mix is cooked – put it in the serving bowls.
12. Enjoy!

Nutritional Information:

calories 257, fat 10g, carbs 34.56g, protein 9g

Butter cauliflower

Servings: 5

Ingredients:

- 1 lb. cauliflower
- ½ c. broccoli
- 1 tbsp. salt
- ¼ c. chicken stock
- 2 garlic cloves
- ½ c. bread crumbs
- 1 tbsp. turmeric
- 3 tbsps. canola oil
- ½ c. parsley
- 4 tbsps. butter
- 2 yellow sweet peppers
- 2 tsps. cream

Directions:

1. Wash the cauliflower carefully and chop it roughly.
2. Put the chopped cauliflower in the instant pot.
3. Add broccoli, salt, chicken stock, turmeric, parsley, and cream.
4. Remove the seeds from the sweet peppers and chop them.
5. Add the peppers in the instant pot too.
6. Peel the garlic cloves and add them in the instant pot.
7. Close the lid and cook the dish at the pressure mode for 18 minutes.
8. When the time is over – strain the liquid and put the vegetables in the blender.
9. Add canola oil and turmeric.
10. Add butter.
11. Sprinkle the mixture with salt and blend it very well.
12. When you get pureed mass – transfer the butter cauliflower in the serving plates.
13. Sprinkle the dish with the breadcrumbs and serve it.
14. Enjoy!

Nutritional Information:

calories 155, fat 9.7g, carbs 15.93g, protein 4g

Chili parsnip

Servings: 8

Ingredients:

- 15 oz. parsnip
- 1 tbsp. chili pepper
- 1 tsp. cayenne pepper
- 2 tbsps. olive oil
- ½ lemon
- 1 tbsp. lemon zest
- ½ c. fresh dill
- 1 tsp. ground black pepper
- 2 garlic cloves
- 1 tsp. kosher salt
- 3 oz. shallot
- 1 c. beef broth

Directions:

1. Wash the parsnip carefully and cut it into the strips.
2. Combine the chili pepper and cayenne pepper together.
3. Add lemon zest and ground black pepper.
4. After this peel the garlic cloves and slice them.
5. Chop the shallot.
6. Combine the sliced garlic cloves and chopped shallot together.
7. Add kosher salt and chili pepper mixture.
8. Then chop the dill and add it to the mixture too.
9. Squeeze the lemon juice into the chili mixture.
10. Sprinkle the parsnip strips with the chili mass and stir it carefully.
11. Then place the parsnip strips in the instant pot and close the lid.
12. Adjust the instant pot for 20 minutes and cook the dish.
13. When the time is over – transfer the cooked meal at the serving plates.
14. Enjoy!

Nutritional Information:

calories 83, fat 3.7g, carbs 12.22g, protein 2g

Snacks and Appetizers

Bacon dates

Servings: 7

Ingredients:

- 7 oz. bacon
- 1 tsp. salt
- ½ tsp. ground black pepper
- ½ tsp. paprika
- ½ tsp. olive oil
- 10 oz. dates
- 1 tsp. butter
- ¼ c. fresh dill

Directions:

1. Slice the bacon and sprinkle it with the salt and ground black pepper.
2. Add paprika and olive oil.
3. Chop the fresh dill and butter together.
4. Fill the dates with the dill-butter mixture.
5. Then wrap the dates in the spicy bacon slices.
6. Then put the bacon dates in the instant pot.
7. Close the lid and cook the dish at the pressure mode for 7 minutes.
8. Then chill the cooked snack little and serve.
9. Enjoy!

Nutritional Information:

calories 212, fat 9.4g, carbs 32.6g, protein 4g

Onion tarts

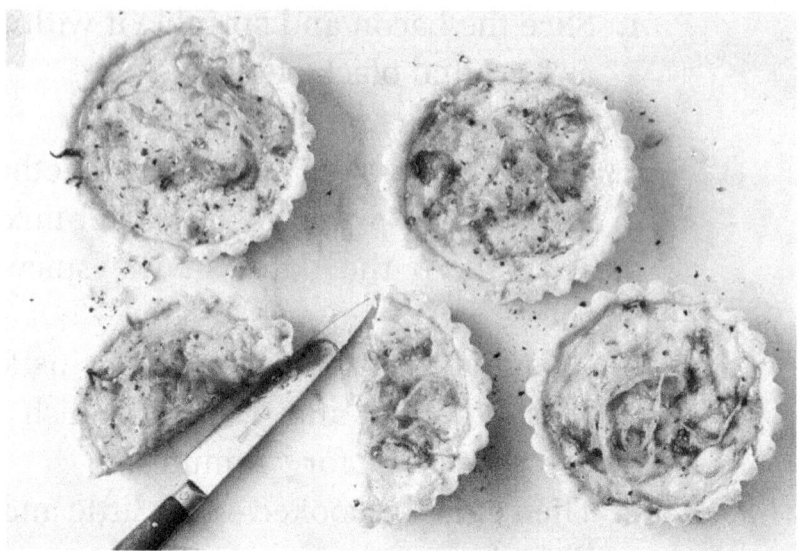

Servings: 5

Ingredients:

- 7 oz. puff pastry
- 1 tsp. ground white pepper
- 7 oz. Cheddar cheese
- 3 white onions
- 1 tsp. salt
- 1 tbsp. butter
- 1 tsp. olive oil
- 3 oz. ground chicken
- 3 oz. black olives

Directions:

1. Roll the puff pastry with the help of the rolling pin.
2. Then slice the black olives.
3. Grate Cheddar cheese.
4. Cut the rolled puff pastry into the middle squares.
5. Then take the muffin forms and spread them with the olive oil.
6. Put the puff pastry squares in the muffin forms.
7. Then peel the onions and dice them.
8. Combine the diced onions with the salt, ground white pepper, and butter.
9. Add the ground chicken and churn the mixture.
10. Put the small amount of the mixture in the muffin forms.
11. Sprinkle the tarts with the grated cheese and transfer them in the instant pot.
12. Cook the tarts at the pressure mode for 16 minutes.
13. Then chill the cooked tarts well and serve them.
14. Enjoy!

Nutritional Information:

calories 389, fat 24.9g, carbs 30.21g, protein 12g

Aromatic palmiers

Servings: 5

Ingredients:

- 6 tbsps. pesto sauce
- 1 tbsp. tomato sauce
- 1 tsp. mayo sauce
- 2 tsps. minced garlic
- 8 oz. puff pastry
- 1 tsp. salt
- 3 eggs
- 1 tsp. heavy cream
- 5 oz. chicken fillet
- 1 c. lettuce
- 1 tsp. butter

Directions:

1. Roll the puff pastry into the thin layer.
2. Combine the tomato sauce, mayo sauce, minced garlic, and salt together.
3. Mix it carefully and spread the puff pastry with the sauce mixture.
4. Peel the eggs and chop them.
5. Chop the chicken filler and lettuce.
6. Combine the chopped eggs with the chicken fillet, and lettuce.
7. Add heavy cream and churn the mass.
8. Make the layer of the lettuce mixture at the puff pastry.
9. Roll the puff pastry carefully.
10. Then cut the rolled puff pastry on the thick rounds.
11. Make the palmiers from the roll with the help of the fingertips.
12. Transfer the palmiers in the instant pot. Spread them with the butter and close the lid.
13. Cook the dish for 20 minutes at the pressure mode.
14. Then chill the cooked dish well and serve it.
15. Enjoy!

Nutritional Information:

calories 523, fat 38.9g, carbs 29.76g, protein 14g

Sausage ring

Servings: 8

Ingredients:

- 1 tsp. yeast
- 1 c. whey
- 2 c. flour
- 1 tsp. sugar
- ½ tsp. salt
- 9 oz. sausages
- 3 oz. bacon
- 3 medium tomatoes
- ½ c. parsley
- 1 tsp. black pepper, ground
- 1 tsp. butter
- 6 oz. Parmesan cheese
- 2 red sweet peppers

Directions:

1. Combine the yeast with the whey and sugar.
2. Add salt and flour.
3. Knead the non-sticky dough.
4. Then roll the dough in the shape of the log.
5. Chop the bacon and parsley.
6. After this, chop the sausages and tomatoes.
7. Grate Parmesan cheese.
8. Remove the seeds from the sweet peppers and chop them.
9. Then combine all the ingredients together and poach the mixture.
10. Spread the dough log with the chopped mixture and brace the dough.
11. Then make the shape of the ring and transfer it to the instant pot.
12. Close the lid and cook the sausage ring for 35 minutes at the pressure mode.
13. When the sausage ring is cooked – chill it little and serve.
14. Enjoy!

Nutritional Information:

calories 350, fat 15.9g, carbs 36.34g, protein 18g

Beef & Lamb

Servings: 4

Ingredients:

- 2 lbs. lamb meat
- 2 tbsps. avocado oil
- 2 diced onions
- 1 tsp. turmeric powder
- 2 tsps. salt
- 1 tsp. cumin powder
- 1 tbsp. coriander powder
- 4 cardamom pods
- 4 whole cloves
- 1 bay leaf
- 3 minced garlic cloves
- 1½ inch knob fresh ginger minced up
- ½ lb. potatoes, halved
- ½ c. water
- 1 tsp. Garam Masala
- 2 cans organic tomatoes, diced
- 1 tsp. paprika
- 1 tsp. Kashmiri chili powder

Directions:

1. Set your instant pot to the sauté mode, add the oil and heat it.
2. Put the meat into the pot and brown it on all sides for 2-minutes per side.
3. Add onion, ginger, spices, garlic, and bay leaf, then stir-fry for 3-minutes.
4. Pour water and diced tomatoes into the pot.
5. Close the lid on the pot and set it to Manual mode, on high, with a cook time of 45-minutes. When the cook time is completed, release the pressure naturally for 10-minutes.
6. Set the pot to the sauté mode to allow the stew to thicken. Serve hot and enjoy!

Nutritional Information:

Calories: 559, Fat: 29g, Carbs: 18g, Protein: 57g

Inspiring Instant Pot Lamb Stew

Servings: 6

Ingredients:

- 2 lbs. lamb stew meat, cubed
- 1 acorn squash
- ¼ tsp. salt
- 6 sliced cloves garlic
- 1 bay leaf
- 2 sprigs rosemary
- 1 large yellow onion
- 3 pieces carrot

Directions:

1. Peel the squash and deseed it, cube the squash. Slice the carrots up into circles.
2. Peel the onion, slice in half and slice the halves into half-moons. Add all the ingredients into instant pot, close and secure pot lid.
3. Set pot to Manual mode, on high, with a cook time of 25-minutes. When the cook time is completed, release the pressure naturally for 10-minutes.
4. Serve warm and enjoy!

Nutritional Information:

Calories: 271, Fat: 20g, Carbs: 5g, Protein: 13g

Instant Pot Lamb Spare Ribs

Servings: 5

Ingredients:

- 2.5 lbs. pastured lamb spare ribs
- 2 tsps. kosher salt
- 1 tbsp. curry powder
  Ingredients for the sauce:
- 1 tbsp. curry powder

- ½ lb. minced garlic
- 1 chopped onion
- 1 tsp. coconut oil
- 4 scallions, thinly sliced
- 1¼ c. divided cilantro
- Juice of 1 lemon
- 1 tbsp. kosher salt

Directions:

1. Add your spare ribs to a bowl. Season them with 2 teaspoons salt, 1 teaspoon of curry powder and mix well.
2. Coat the ribs thoroughly with the mix. Cover them up and allow them to chill for 4 hours. Set your instant pot to the sauté mode, add oil and let it heat.
3. Add the spare ribs and brown them on both sides for 2-minutes per side. Transfer to another plate. Take a blender and add onion, tomato and blend into a paste.
4. Add minced garlic to your pot, keep stirring as you add the paste to it. Add curry powder, chopped cilantro, lemon juice and salt. Let the mixture reach a boil and stir in the ribs.
5. Close and secure the lid to the pot, set it at Manual mode, on high, with a cook time of 20-minutes.
6. When the cook time is completed, release the pressure naturally for 10-minutes. Serve warm.

Nutritional Information:

Calories: 165, Fats: 14g, Carbs: 5g, protein: 10g

Lamb & Avocado Salad

Servings: 10

Ingredients:

- 1 pitted avocado
- 1 c. lettuce
- 1 tbsp. sesame oil
- 1 tsp. basil
- 1 garlic clove
- 3 tbsps. olive oil
- 1 tsp. chili pepper
- 1 tsp. salt
- 3 c. water
- 8 oz. lamb fillet
- 1 cucumber

Directions:

1. Place the lamb fillet in the instant pot and add the water.
2. Sprinkle some salt into the pot. Add peeled garlic clove to the lamb mixture.
3. Close the lid to pot and cook on MEAT mode for 35-minutes.
4. Chop the avocado and slice the cucumber. Combine these ingredients in a mixing bowl.
5. Roughly chop the lettuce and add it to the mixing bowl. Now, sprinkle the mixture with the chili pepper, basil, olive oil and sesame oil. When the meat is done cooking—remove it from your instant pot and chill.
6. Chop the meat roughly and add it to the mixing bowl. Mix up the salad carefully and transfer to serving bowl.
7. Serve warm.

Nutritional Information:

Calories: 276, Fat: 6g, Carbs: 3g, Protein: 21g

Italian Lamb Shanks

Servings: 4

Ingredients:

- 3 lbs. lamb shanks
- 4 minced cloves garlic
- 3 diced stalks celery
- 1 c. beef stock
- 1 tbsp. balsamic vinegar
- 1 tbsp. coconut oil
- 1 tbsp. tomato paste
- 1 diced yellow onion
- ½ tsp. crushed red pepper flakes
- ½ tsp. salt
- ¼ tsp. black pepper
- 14 oz. fire-roasted tomatoes
- 3 carrots, peeled and chopped
- Italian parsley, freshly choppe

Directions:

1. Sprinkle lamb shanks with pepper and salt.
2. Set your instant pot to the sautė mode, add the coconut oil and heat. Add the lamb shanks to hot coconut oil and cook for about 10-minutes or until all sides are brown. Transfer to a platter when sides are browned.
3. Add garlic, celery, onion, and carrots to instant pot. Use salt and pepper to season, cook until the onion becomes translucent— stirring often. Add the fire-roasted tomatoes and tomato paste.
4. Stir to blend. Return the lamb shanks to the pot. Add the beef stock and balsamic vinegar.
5. Cancel the sautė mode, and cover pot with lid and secure it. Set the pot to Manual mode, on high, with a cook time of 45-minutes.
6. When the cook time is completed, release the pressure naturally for 15-minutes. Transfer the lamb shanks to a serving plate. Ladle sauce over lamb shanks.
7. Garnish with fresh, chopped parsley and enjoy warm!

Nutritional Information:

Calories: 257, Fat: 11g, Carbs: 9g, Protein: 28g

Ground Lamb Curry

Servings: 4

Ingredients:

- 1 lb. ground lamb
- ½ tsp. Kashmiri chili powder
- ½ tsp. cumin powder
- 1 tsp. salt
- 1 tsp. paprika
- 1 tsp. meat masala, homemade
- 1 tbsp. coriander powder
- 1 diced onion
- 1 c. frozen peas, rinsed
- 2 chopped potatoes
- 13.5 oz. tomato sauce
- 3 chopped carrots
- 4 chopped tomatoes
- 4 minced garlic cloves
- 2 tbsps. ghee
- 1-inch freshly minced ginger
- 2 Serrano peppers, minced
- ¼ tsp. turmeric powder
- ½ tsp. black pepper
- Freshly chopped cilantro

Directions:

1. Set your instant pot to the sauté mode, add the ghee and heat it.
2. Add onions and cook them until they start to brown.
3. Add the garlic, ginger, Serrano pepper and stir-fry for 1-minute. Add the tomatoes.
4. Cook for 5-minutes, then add the spice and stir-fry for 1-minute. Add the ground lamb and cook until the meat is browned.
5. Add the potatoes, carrots, peas, and tomato sauce.
6. Mix well until combined. Press the CANCEL button to stop the sauté mode. Cover and secure the lid to the pot. Press the CHILI button and cook for 30-minutes.
7. When the instant pot completes the cooking, release the pressure naturally for 15-minutes.
8. Carefully open the lid and serve dish warm.

Nutritional Information:

Calories: 267, Fat: 8g, Carbs: 12g, Protein: 27g

Rosemary Lamb

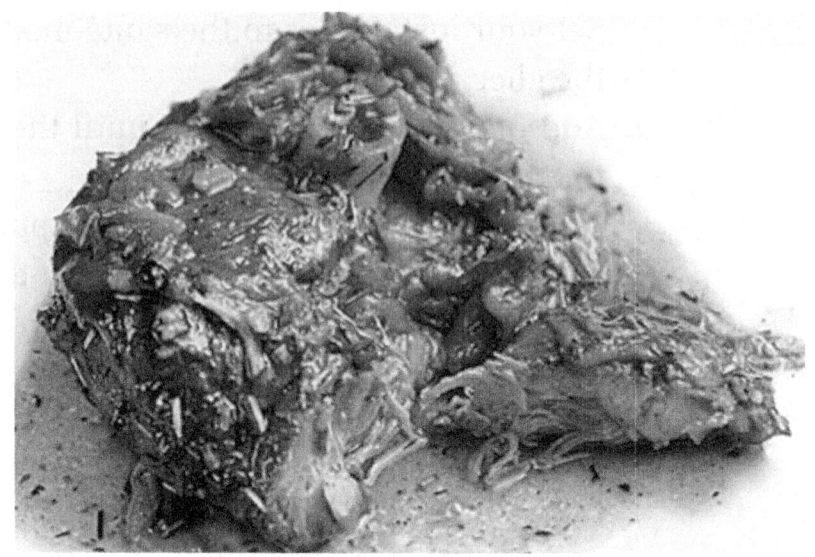

Servings: 6

Ingredients:

- 4 lbs. lamb, cubed, boneless
- 1 c. sliced carrots
- 2 tbsps. olive oil
- 3 tbsps. flour
- 6 rosemary sprigs
- 4 minced garlic cloves
- Salt and pepper
- 1½ c. veggie stock

Directions:

1. Set your instant pot to the sauté mode, add the oil and heat.
2. Season the lamb with salt and pepper. Place lamb inside the pot with minced garlic. Cook until the lamb has browned all over.
3. Add the flour and stir, slowly pour in the stock. Add the rosemary and carrots, close and secure the pot lid.
4. Set to Manual mode, on high, with a cook time of 20-minutes. When the cook time is completed, release the pressure naturally for 10-minutes. Remove the rosemary stems from the pot.
5. Serve lamb with plenty of sauce.

Nutritional Information:

Calories: 272, Fat: 11g, Carbs: 9g, Protein: 29g

Thyme Lamb

Servings: 8

Ingredients:

- 1 c. fresh thyme
- 2 lbs. lamb
- 1 tsp. oregano
- 1 tbsp. olive oil
- 1 tbsp. turmeric
- ¼ c. chicken stock
- 4 tbsps. butter
- 1 tsp. sugar
- ¼ c. rice wine
- 1 tsp. paprika
- 1 tbsp. ground black pepper

Directions:

1. Chop the fresh thyme and combine it with the oregano, ground black pepper, paprika, sugar, rice wine, chicken stock, and turmeric, mix well.
2. Sprinkle the lamb with the spice mixture and stir carefully. Transfer the lamb mixture to your instant pot and add olive oil to the pot.
3. Close the instant pot and secure the lid, set on MEAT mode for 45-minutes.
4. When the cooking is completed, release the pressure naturally for 10-minutes.
5. Chill the lamb for a little bit before you slice it. Serve warm or cold.

Nutritional Information:

Calories: 282, Fat: 12g, Carbs: 8g, Protein: 28g

Garlic Lamb Shanks with Port

Servings: 4

Ingredients:

- 4 lbs. lamb shanks
- 1 c. port wine
- 1 c. chicken broth
- 1 tsp. dried rosemary
- 2 tsps. balsamic vinegar
- 2 tbsps. ghee
- 2 tbsps. tomato paste
- 20 peeled, whole garlic cloves
- Salt and pepper

Directions:

1. Trim any excess fat from lamb that you do not want, and season it generously with salt and pepper.
2. Heat oil in your instant pot on the sauté mode.
3. Place the lamb into the pot, and brown it all over.
4. Pour in the port and stock, stir in the tomato paste and rosemary.
5. When the tomato paste is dissolved, close and secure the pot lid.
6. Set to Manual mode, on high, with a cook time of 32-minutes.
7. When the cook time is completed, release the pressure naturally for 10-minutes.
8. Remove the lamb from pot and set the pot back onto the sauté mode for about 5-minutes to thicken the sauce.
9. Add in vinegar and mix well. Serve with the sauce poured over the lamb.

Nutritional Information:

Calories: 298, Fat: 13g, Carbs: 11g, Protein: 26g

Lamb & Feta Meatballs

Servings: 6

Ingredients:

- 1½ lbs. ground lamb
- 4 minced garlic cloves
- 28 oz. crushed tomatoes
- 2 tbsps. olive oil
- 2 tbsps. chopped parsley
- ½ c. breadcrumbs
- ½ c. crumbled feta cheese
- 1 chopped onion
- 1 chopped green bell pepper
- 1 egg
- 6 oz. tomato sauce
- ¼ tsp. black pepper
- ½ tsp. salt
- 1 tsp. dried oregano
- 1 tbsp. water
- 1 tbsp. mint, freshly chopped

Directions:

1. In a bowl, mix breadcrumbs, egg, lamb, mint, parsley, feta, water, half of the minced garlic, pepper and salt. Mold into 1-inch balls using your hands.
2. Set your instant pot to the sauté mode, add oil and heat.
3. Add the onion and bell pepper to hot oil and cook for 2-minutes before the rest of the garlic.
4. After about 1-minute add the crushed tomatoes with their liquid, the tomato sauce, and oregano.
5. Sprinkle with salt and pepper.
6. Close and secure the pot lid, select Manual mode, on high, with a cook time of 8-minutes.
7. When the cook time is completed, release the pressure using quick-release.
8. Serve the meatballs with parsley and more cheese!

Nutritional Information:

Calories: 302, Fat: 14g, Carbs: 12g, Protein: 30g

Braised Lamb Shanks with Carrots & Tomatoes

Servings: 4

Ingredients:

- 2 lbs. lamb shanks
- 2 carrots, peeled and sliced
- 2 c. whole canned tomatoes, sliced
- 6 tbsps. olive oil
- 6 sliced cloves garlic
- 3 sprigs fresh thyme, chopped
- 3 sprigs fresh rosemary, chopped
- 3 sprigs fresh oregano, chopped
- 1 white onion, large
- 1½ c. veal stock or beef stock
- Flour for dredging
- Salt and pepper

Directions:

1. Set your instant pot to the sauté mode.
2. Dredge lamb shanks with flour and cook in the pot until all sides are browned. When the lamb shanks are browned, add all the ingredients in the pot, except for the canned tomatoes.
3. Cancel the sauté mode, and close and secure the pot lid. Set the pot to Manual mode, on high, with a cook time of 25-minutes. When the cook time is completed, release the pressure naturally for 15-minutes.
4. Open the pot and add the canned tomatoes and stir. Cover and secure the lid again and set on Manual, on high, with a 5-minute cook time.
5. When the cooking is completed, use the quick-release.
6. Pour the gravy from the pot over the lamb shanks and other food and enjoy!

Nutritional Information:

Calories: 304, Fat: 15g, Carbs: 10g, Protein: 32g

Ginger-Spiced Lamb Shanks with Figs

Servings: 6

Ingredients:

- 4 (12 oz.) lamb shanks
- 1½ c. bone broth
- 2 tsps. fish sauce
- 2 tbsps. apple cider vinegar
- 2 tbsps. ginger, fresh, minced
- 2 tbsps. coconut Aminos
- 2 tbsps. coconut oil
- 1 sliced onion
- 3 garlic cloves, minced
- 10 halved and stemmed figs, dried
- Salt and pepper

Directions:

1. Set your instant pot to the sauté mode, add 1 tablespoon oil and heat.
2. Add the lamb into pot and brown on all sides. You might have to do 2 at a time and add more coconut oil.
3. Place all the lamb shanks on a platter after they are browned. Add the onion and ginger to pot and stir for 3-minutes.
4. Add the fish sauce, vinegar, coconut Aminos, and minced garlic. Pour the broth in and add the figs; deglazing any stuck-on meat or onions.
5. Place the meat back into the pot and close the lid. Set to Manual mode, on high, with a cook time of 60-minutes.
6. When the cook time is completed, release the pressure naturally for 30-minutes.
7. Remove shanks from pot placing them onto serving plates. Add the sauce over the lamb shanks, serve and enjoy!

Nutritional Information:

Calories: 306, Fat: 15g, Carbs: 13g, Protein: 31g

Lamb & Feta Cocktail Meatballs

Servings: 10

Ingredients:

- 2 crushed garlic cloves
- 2 lbs. ground lamb meat
- ½ lb. feta cheese, crumbled
- 1 egg
- ½ c. breadcrumbs
- 2 tbsps. chopped parsley
- 1 tbsp. fresh mint, chopped
- ½ tsp. kosher salt, plus more for sauce
- 1 tbsp. Worcestershire sauce

Directions:

1. In a large mixing bowl, add lamb, garlic, feta, egg, breadcrumbs, parsley, mint, salt, pepper and Worcestershire sauce.
2. Form mixture into 1-inch balls and place them in the freezer; allow them to harden for a few hours.
3. Add 1 cup water and steamer basket to your instant pot. Lower the frozen meatballs onto the steamer basket. Close and secure the lid to the pot. Set on Manual mode, on high, with a cook time of 5-minutes.
4. When the cook time is completed, release the pressure using the quick-release.
5. Serve meatballs on a serving platter, serve with cocktail picks and one of your special sauces.

Nutritional Information:

Calories: 258, Fat: 11.2g, Carbs: 5.3g, Protein: 32.2g

Beef Stroganoff

Servings: 4

Ingredients:

- 2 c. beef strip
- ¼ tsp. pepper
- ¼ tsp. salt
- 1½ c. zucchini noodles
- 2 c. beef broth
- 3 tbsps. Worcestershire sauce
- 2 tbsps. tomato paste
- 1 c. sliced mushroom
- 2 minced garlic cloves
- 1 chopped onion
- 1 tbsp. almond flour
- 3 tbsps. olive oil

Directions:

1. In a bowl mix the beef strips, flour, salt, and pepper.
2. Coat the beef strips with flour and seasoning.
3. Set your instant pot on low heat and low pressure, with a cook time of 10-minutes.
4. Cook your meat for 10-minutes.
5. Place the remaining ingredients into the pot and set for an additional 18-minutes.
6. When the cook time is completed, release the pressure naturally for 10 minutes.
7. Serve with some zoodles.

Nutritional Information:

Calories: 335, Fat: 18g, Carbs: 12g, Protein: 20.02g

Vietnamese Bo Kho

Servings: 4

Ingredients:

- ½ tsp. ghee
- 2½ lbs. beef brisket
- 1 diced yellow onion, peeled
- 1 ½ tsps. curry powder
- 2½ tbsps. peeled fresh ginger
- 2 c. drained, crushed, diced tomatoes
- 3 tbsps. fish sauce
- 2 tbsps. applesauce
- 1 large stalk of lemongrass, chopped
- 2 whole star anise
- 1 bay leaf
- 1 c. bone broth

Directions:

1. Set your instant pot to the sauté mode, add ghee and heat it.
2. Add briskets and fry until they have a nice brown texture.
3. Remove the brisket and keep it on the side.
4. Add onion, sauté, add the curry powder, seared beef, fish sauce, ginger, diced tomatoes, star anise.
5. Pour the applesauce and stir well. Add the bay leaf and lemongrass.
6. Pour broth and lock up the lid, set on Manual, on high, with a cook time of 35-minutes.
7. When cook time is completed, release the pressure naturally for 10-minutes.
8. Add carrots to pot and close and secure lid again, cook on high for 7-minutes.
9. Release the pressure using quick-release, then serve and enjoy!

Nutritional Information:

Calories: 462, Fat: 20g, Carbs: 15g, Protein: 26g

Beef Bourguignon

Servings: 4

Ingredients:

- 1 lb. stewing steak
- ½ lb. bacon
- 1 tbsp. olive oil
- ½ c. beef broth
- 2 tsps. ground black pepper
- 2 tbsps. Freshly chopped parsley
- 2 tbsps. fresh thyme
- 2 tsps. rock salt
- 2 minced garlic cloves
- 1 red onion, peeled and sliced
- 5 medium carrots

Directions:

1. Set your instant pot to the sauté mode, add 1 tablespoon of olive oil.
2. Allow oil to heat, and then add the beef and brown it.
3. Slice the cooked bacon into strips alongside the onion in your pot.
4. Add remaining ingredients and stir.
5. Close and secure the lid, set on Manual, on high, for a cook time of 30-minutes.
6. When the cook time is completed, release the pressure naturally for 10-minutes. Serve warm and enjoy!

Nutritional Information:

Calories: 416, Fat: 18g, Carbs: 12g, Protein: 29g

Instant Pot Beef Stew

Servings: 6

Ingredients:

- 16 oz. tenderloin cut
- 1 chopped onion
- 3 Yukon gold potatoes, chopped
- 1 chopped zucchini
- 1 c. chopped carrots
- 2 c. beef broth
- 2 tsps. sea salt
- 1 bay leaf
- 1 tbsp. tomato paste
- 1 tsp. onion powder
- 1 tsp. paprika
- 1 tsp. pepper
- 2 tbsps. arrowroot flour
- Worcestershire sauce

Directions:

1. Set your instant pot to the sauté mode, add the oil and heat it.
2. Add the tenderloin in the oil.
3. Saute them until the meat is well cooked and no longer pink.
4. Add the vegetables and stir in the broth, with seasoning.
5. Close and secure the lid, set to STEW/MEAT mode, with a cook time of 35-minutes.
6. Once cook time is completed, release the pressure naturally for 10-minutes.
7. Ladle ¼ of the liquid into a bowl and mix arrowroot flour with it, making a slurry.
8. Add the slurry back into the instant pot and stir.
9. Season a bit with salt, serve hot and enjoy!

Nutritional Information:

Calories: 310, Fat: 8g, Carbs: 18g, Protein: 39g

Simple Beef Short Ribs

Servings: 5

Ingredients:

- 4lbs. beef short ribs
- 1 tbsp. beef fat
- 3 cloves garlic
- ½ c. water
- 1 quartered onion
- Kosher salt

Directions:

1. Season the beef ribs with salt all over.
2. In a skillet over medium heat add oil and allow it to heat up.
3. Add the ribs to skillet and brown them. Add the onion, garlic, and water.
4. Transfer the mixture to your instant pot and stir. Close and secure the lid, set on Manual mode, on high, with a cook time of 35-minutes.
5. Release the pressure naturally for 10-minutes. Serve warm.

Nutritional Information:

Calories: 440, Fat: 41g, Carbs: 10g, Protein: 27g

Beef Goulash

Servings: 6

Ingredients:

- 2 lbs. extra lean ground beef
- 2 tbsps. sweet paprika
- 1 tbsp. minced garlic
- 1 onion, chopped
- 1 chopped red bell pepper, stemmed and seeded
- 2 tsps. olive oil
- 2 cans diced petite tomatoes
- 4 c. beef stock
- ½ tsp. hot paprika

Directions:

1. Set to your sauté mode and add 2 tablespoons olive oil.
2. Add ground beef to the pot and keep cooking and stirring until it breaks.
3. Once the beef is browned, transfer it to another bowl.
4. Slice the stem of the pepper and deseed them. Cut them into strips.
5. Cut the onions into short strips.
6. Add teaspoon olive oil to the pot and add onion and pepper. Add minced garlic, sweet paprika, and cook for 3-minutes.
7. Add beef stock and tomatoes. Add ground beef and close and secure the lid, cook on low pressure for 15-minutes on the SOUP mode.
8. Use the quick-release when cooking is completed. Serve hot and enjoy!

Nutritional Information:

Calories: 283, Fat: 13g, Carbs: 14g, Protein: 30g

Instant Pot Korean Beef

Servings: 6

Ingredients:

- 4lbs. roast, chopped
- ¼ tsp. salt
- ¼ tsp. black pepper
- 1 c. chicken broth
- 4 tbsps. soy sauce
- ¼ tsp. garlic paste
- ¼ tsp. ginger
- 1 chopped pear
- 2 c. orange juice
- 1 tbsp. honey

Directions:

1. Trim extra fat off the roast, rinse and fully dry.
2. Season roast with salt and pepper. Set aside.
3. Set the instant pot to the sauté mode, add olive oil and heat it. Add the meat to pot and brown on all sides for about 5-minutes.
4. Remove meat from pot and set aside. In the instant pot pour orange juice, soy sauce, garlic, ginger, pear and honey and stir to blend.
5. Cover up the instant pot with lid and set to Manual mode, on high, for a cook time of 45-minutes.
6. When cook time is completed, release the pressure naturally for 15-minutes.
7. Shred the meat using two forks, then serve with rice and enjoy!

Nutritional Information:

Calories: 490, Fat: 24g, Carbs: 26g, Protein: 41g

Beef Ragu

Servings: 6

Ingredients:

- 18 oz. beef chunks
- 2 tbsps. Chopped parsley
- 2 bay leaves
- 2 sprigs fresh thyme
- 7 oz. roasted red peppers
- 28 oz. crushed tomatoes
- 5 smashed garlic cloves
- 1 tsp. olive oil
- Black pepper
- 1 tsp. salt

Directions:

1. Season the beef with salt and pepper. Set your instant pot to the sauté mode, add the oil and heat it.
2. Cook the garlic in a pot and turn to brown. It will take about 2-minutes, then remove garlic with slotted spoon.
3. Put the beef in the instant pot and cook a couple of minutes on each side. Add remaining ingredients to the pot.
4. Keep half of the parsley for later for garnish. Cook the beef on manual mode, on high, for a cook time of 45-minutes.
5. When the cook time is completed, release the pressure naturally for 10-minutes. Remove the bay leaves and discard them.
6. Shred the beef using two forks. Garnish beef with remaining parsley and serve hot with some pasta.

Nutritional Information:

Calories: 298, Fat: 11g, Carbs: 14g, Protein: 29g

Sloppy Joe with Beef

Servings: 6

Ingredients:

- 2 lbs. ground beef
- 2 tbsps. yellow mustard
- 2 tbsps. molasses
- 2 tbsps. apple cider vinegar
- 15 oz. tomato sauce
- ½ tsp. black pepper
- 1 tsp. pepper
- 1 tsp. cayenne
- 2 tsps. salt
- 2 tsps. paprika
- 2 tsps. smoked paprika
- 2 tsps. cumin
- 8 minced garlic cloves
- 2 diced onions
- 2 tbsps. olive oil
- Chopped cilantro

Directions:

1. Set your instant pot to the sauté mode, add oil and heat it.

2. Sauté, the onions in the oil for 5-minutes, then add the garlic, spices and ground beef. Cook thoroughly until the beef turns brown. Add all the remaining ingredients, stir.

3. Close the lid to pot and set on the BEAN/CHILI mode, make sure the steam valve is closed.

4. After 30-minutes the cook time will be completed, release the pressure naturally for 10-minutes. Serve hot.

Nutritional Information:

Calories: 304, Fat: 12g, Carbs: 16g, Protein: 28g

Beef & Tomato Soup

Servings: 6

Ingredients:

- 1 lb. ground beef
- 1 tbsp. olive oil
- 1 chopped onion
- Black pepper
- 15 oz. beef broth
- 15 oz. diced tomatoes
- 1 tsp. dried oregano
- 1 tsp. thyme, dried
- 1 tbsp. minced garlic

Directions:

1. Turn your instant pot to the sauté mode, add the oil and heat it. Add the beef to pot and cook it until it turns brown.
2. Add the onion, thyme, oregano, garlic and cook for an additional 3-minutes.
3. Add the tomatoes and beef broth and close the pot lid. Set to SOUP mode and cook for 30-minutes.
4. When cooking is completed, release the pressure using the quick-release. Season with salt and pepper. Serve the soup warm.

Nutritional Information:

Calories: 302, Fat: 15g, Carbs: 14g, Protein: 30g

Beef Chili

Servings: 10

Ingredients:

- 2 lbs. ground beef
- 2 tbsps. olive oil
- 1 tsp. black pepper
- 2 tsps. salt
- 1 tbsp. cumin
- 1 tbsp. oregano
- 2 tbsps. chili powder
- 14 oz. diced tomatoes
- 2 minced jalapenos
- 2 chopped bell peppers
- 5 chopped celery stalks
- 8 chopped carrots
- 10 minced garlic cloves
- 2 diced red onions
- ¼ tsp. cayenne

Directions:

1. Set your instant pot on the sauté mode, add the oil and heat it.
2. Place the onion and garlic and cook them for 2-minutes.
3. Add the beef to pot, making sure to brown beef, then add remaining ingredients to the pot and cover with lid.
4. Press the 'Keep Warm or Cancel Button and then press the BEAN/CHILI button to begin cooking.
5. It will automatically cook your food for 30-minutes. When the cooking is done, the pot will automatically switch to the Keep Warm mode.
6. Release the pressure naturally for 15-minutes. Serve warm.

Nutritional Information:

Calories: 306, Fat: 12g, Carbs: 9g, Protein: 32g

Beef Curry

Servings: 6

Ingredients:

- 1 can coconut milk
- 1 tsp. lemon zest
- 4lbs. beef cubes
- ½ tsp. salt
- 1 tsp. turmeric
- 1 tbsp. curry powder
- ¼ c. lemon juice

Directions:

1. Add the liquid of the coconut milk into mixing bowl, add lemon juice, lemon zest, and all the spices to make the marinade mixture.
2. Now coat the beef pieces thoroughly with this mixture and keep aside.
3. Pour half portion of coconut milk at the bottom of the instant pot, then add the marinated beef to pot.
4. Pour the remaining part of coconut milk into a pot, then close the lid. Set instant pot to the POULTRY setting and on a cook time of 20-minutes.
5. When the cook time is completed, release the pressure using quick-release. Serve the beef warm as a side dish.

Nutritional Information:

Calories: 297, Fat: 11g, Carbs: 8g, Protein: 26g

Saucy Beef

Servings: 3

Ingredients:

- 6 medium beef cubes
- 1 tbsp. cider vinegar
- 1.5 c. tomatillo sauce
- 1 tsp. olive oil
- 1 tsp. oregano, dried
- 1/8 tsp. black pepper
- 1 tsp. kosher salt
- ¼ c. chopped cilantro
- 1 jalapeno, halved and seeded

Directions:

1. Season the beef with salt, pepper, vinegar, oregano and marinate for 2 hours.
2. Set the instant pot to the sauté mode and add oil. Cook beef till it turns brown. After cooking beef, add all the other ingredients (except cilantro).
3. Set to Manual mode, on high, with a cook time of 20-minutes. When the cook time is completed, release the pressure naturally for 10-minutes.
4. Before serving garnish with cilantro.

Nutritional Information:

Calories: 296, Fat: 12g, Carbs: 10g, Protein: 31g

Beef Stock

Servings: 8

Ingredients:

- 2.5 lbs. beef, bones in
- 1 chopped carrot
- ½ tsp. black pepper
- 1 tsp. kosher salt
- 1 sprig fresh parsley
- 1 bay leaf
- 1 leek, only the green trimmings
- 1 small shallot
- 1 chopped celery rib
- 10 c. water

Directions:

1. Add beef to your instant pot and then put all vegetables and herbs over the bones.
2. Add the salt and pepper and finally pour 10 cups of water into the pot. Set the instant pot on the SEALING mode.
3. Set the cook time for 60-minutes. When the cook time is completed, release the pressure using quick-release.
4. Remove the lid of the pot and allow the stock to cool down, then strain the stock to get the clear liquid. Serve warm.

Nutritional Information:

Calories: 302, Fat: 13g, Carbs: 16g, Protein: 24g

Pork

Kalua Pig

Servings: 8

Ingredients:

- 6 lbs. pork roast, sliced
- 4 bacon slices
- 3 garlic cloves
- 1 c. water
- 1 tbsp. salt
- 1 cabbage, cut into wedges

Directions:

1. Set your instant pot to the sauté setting, and cook bacon slices for about 1-minute, cooking and browning all sides. Sprinkle salt on pork.
2. Spread the salt on bacon evenly. Pour water into the instant pot and set to Manual mode.
3. Cover pot with lid and set on high with a cook time of 90-minutes.
4. When the cook time is completed set the pot to the "Keep Warm" mode and release the pressure naturally for 10-minutes.
5. Place the cooked pork in a bowl, taste the remaining liquid in the instant pot. Adjust seasoning as needed.
6. Now chop the cabbage and add it to the instant pot into the cooking liquid. Cover the pot once again and set on high with a cook time of 5-minutes.
7. When the cook time is completed, release pressure using quick-release. Serve the shredded pork with the cooked cabbage.

Nutritional Information:

Calories: 783, Fat: 1g, Carbs: 40g, Protein: 5g

Pulled Apart Pork Carnitas

Servings: 6

Ingredients:

- 4 lbs. pork roast
- 2 tbsps. olive oil
- 1 head butter lettuce
- 2 grated carrots
- 2 limes, wedge cut
- Water

For the spice mixture

- 1 tbsp. salt
- 1 tbsp. cocoa
- 1 tbsp. red pepper flakes
- 1 tsp. cumin
- 1 tsp. garlic
- 1 tsp. white pepper
- 2 tsps. oregano
- 1 onion, chopped
- 1/8 tsp. cayenne pepper
- 1/8 tsp. coriander

Directions:

1. Add the "spice" ingredients in a bowl and mix them well. Season the roast with the prepared mixture and chill the roast in your fridge overnight.
2. Set your instant pot to the sauté mode and add the olive oil and heat it. Add the meat and brown it well.
3. Add water to the instant pot to submerge meat (about 1 cup). Secure the lid of the pot in place, and set to Manual mode, on high with a cook time of 60-minutes.
4. When the cook time is completed, release the pressure naturally for 15-minutes.
5. Remove the meat from pot and shred the meat from bones. Set your instant pot to sauté mode, simmer to reduce some of the liquid.
6. Add the shredded pork to a pan set over medium heat and stir-fry them until slightly browned.
7. Add some olive oil and spices. Serve fried pork with the sauce from instant pot.

Nutritional Information:

Calories: 176, Fat: 7g, Carbs: 1.3g, Protein: 5g

Servings: 6

Ingredients:

- 1 c. cubed pineapple
- Olive oil
- Your desired seasoning
- Balsamic glaze
- 6 pork chops, bone-in

Directions:

1. Season the pork chops. Set your instant pot onto the sauté mode. Add the oil and heat it.
2. Add the chops to the pot and sauté them for a 5-minutes.
3. Remove the chops and place them onto a steamer rack for instant pot.
4. Glaze the pork chops and place the pineapple chunks on top of them. Add a cup of water into the instant pot.
5. Secure the lid to pot and set to Manual mode, on high with a cook time of 25 minutes.
6. When the cook time is completed, release the pressure naturally for 10-minutes.

Nutritional Information:

Calories: 621, Fat: 15g, Carbs: 101g, Protein: 24g

Apple Pork Tenderloins

Servings: 4

Ingredients:

- 3 lbs. boneless pork loin roast
- 2 tbsps. butter
- 1 red onion, sliced
- ½ tsp. ground black pepper
- ½ tsp. salt
- ¼ c. chicken broth
- 2 bay leaves
- 4 thyme sprigs, fresh
- 2 sliced green apples

Directions:

1. Set your instant pot to the sauté mode, add the butter and heat it.
2. Add the tenderloin pieces and cook them for 8-minutes. Remove the cooked loins to a serving platter.
3. Place the red onion slices into the pot and sauté for 3-minutes. Stir in the bay leaves, thyme, and apple slices.
4. Add broth along with pepper and salt, stir. Add the loins back to the pot. Secure the pot lid and set on Manual mode on high with a cook time of 30-minutes.
5. When the cook time is completed, release the pressure naturally for 10 minutes.
6. Discard the bay leaves and transfer the pork to a cutting board and allow it to sit for 5-minutes. Serve pork with sauce from pot.

Nutritional Information:

Calories: 123, Fat: 45g, Carbs: 43g, Protein: 21g

Pork Shoulder Meal

Servings: 6

Ingredients:

- 3 lbs. boneless pork shoulder, cubed
- ¼ c. orange juice
- ¼ c. lime juice
- 5 minced garlic cloves
- ½ tsp. ground cumin
- 1 tsp. salt
- Chopped cilantro

Directions:

1. Add your lime juice, orange juice, cumin, garlic, and salt to your instant pot and stir to blend.

2. Place the pork into the instant pot and toss to mix. Secure the lid to pot and set to Manual mode, on high with a cook time of 45-minutes.

3. When the cook time is completed, release the pressure naturally for 10-minutes.

4. Pre-heat your grill, using tongs take your pork out of the instant pot and place it on a baking sheet. Set the instant pot to the sauté mode and cook for 10-minutes to allow liquid to reduce.

5. Pour the liquid into a heat-proof dish.

6. Broil the pork for 5-minutes or until crispy and serve with sauce, garnish with fresh cilantro.

Nutritional Information:

Calories: 378, Fat: 19g, Carbs: 1g, Protein: 48g

Yummy Pork Chop

Servings: 4

Ingredients:

- 4 pieces bone-in pork loin or rib chops, ½ inch thick
- 2 tbsps. clarified butter
- ½ c. chicken broth
- ½ c. white grape juice
- 1 tbsp. minced fresh dill fronds
- 16 baby carrots
- Salt and black pepper
- 1 tbsp. ghee

Directions:

1. Set your instant pot to sauté mode. Season pork chop with salt and pepper.
2. Add the chop to the instant pot and cook for 4-minutes. Cook chops in batches if needed, transferring them to a plate.
3. Add 1 tablespoon of ghee to the pot along with carrots, dill and cook for 1-minute.
4. Add a ½ cup of grape juice and deglaze the pot. Stir in the broth and add in the chops. Shut the lid on the pot, and set to Manual mode, on high with a cook time of 18-minutes.
5. When the cook time is completed, release the pressure naturally for 10-minutes. Serve by pouring the cooking sauce over the chops.

Nutritional Information:

Calories: 296, Fat: 25g, Carbs: 0g, Protein: 17g

Cuban Pork Meal

Servings: 10

Ingredients:

- 3 lbs. boneless pork shoulder blade roast, fat trimmed and removed
- Chopped cilantro, fresh
- Lime wedges
- 1 bay leaf
- Salt
- Juice of 1 lime
- ½ tbsp. cumin
- ½ tbsp. fresh oregano
- 2/3 c. grapefruit juice
- 6 garlic cloves
- Hot sauce
- Salsa

Directions:

1. Cut the pork into four pieces, then transfer them to a bowl.
2. Using a hand blender, blend garlic cloves, oregano, lime, grapefruit juice, salt, cumin to form a marinade.
3. Pour this marinade over your pork and allow it to rest for 60-minutes. Transfer this mix to your instant pot and add in a bay leaf.
4. Close and secure the lid and set to Manual mode, on high for 80-minute cook time.
5. When the cook time is completed, release the pressure naturally for 15-minutes. Remove pork from pot and shred it. Return pork to pot and add 1 cup of water and season with some liquid.
6. Set pot to the sauté mode for 4-minutes. Serve warm and garnish with chopped fresh cilantro.

Nutritional Information:

Calories: 213, Fat: 9g, Carbs: 2g, Protein: 26g

Artichoke & Lemon Pork Chops

Servings: 4

Ingredients:

- 2 pieces bone-in pork loin or rib chops, 2-inch thick
- 2 tbsps. ghee
- 3 oz. pancetta, diced chunks
- 2 tsps. ground black pepper
- 1 minced shallot
- 4 pieces lemon zest strips

- 1 tsp. dried rosemary
- 2 tsps. minced garlic
- 1 portion of a 9 oz. box of frozen artichoke heart quarters
- ¼ c. chicken broth
- ½ c. white grape juice

Directions:

1. Set your instant pot to the sauté mode, add the pancetta and cook for 5-minutes.
2. Transfer the browned-up pancetta to a plate. Season the pork chops with pepper and transfer them to your instant pot.
3. Cook the chops for 5-minutes, or until browned, and then remove to a plate. Add the shallots and cook for 1-minute.
4. Add lemon zest, garlic, rosemary, and stir to release a pleasant aroma. Add the chicken broth and artichokes and transfer the pancetta back also. Transfer the chops back into the pot as well.
5. Close and secure the lid to pot and set to Manual mode, on high for a cook time of 24-minutes.
6. When the cook time has completed, release the pressure naturally for 10-minutes.
7. Place the chops on a carving board and slice the meat into strips. Divide into serving bowls, and top with cooking sauce from pot.

Nutritional Information:

Calories: 245, Fat: 45g, Carbs: 12g, Protein: 48g

Pork Loin Chops with Pears

Servings: 4

Ingredients:

- 2 tbsps. ghee
- 4 pieces bone-in pork loin or rib chops, ½ inch thick
- ½ tsp. ground allspice
- ½ c. pear cider, unsweetened
- 2 large Bosc pears, peeled, cored and chopped
- 2 chopped yellow onions
- Salt and black pepper
- Several dashes of hot pepper

Directions:

1. First set your instant pot to the sautė mode, add the ghee and heat it. Toss your pork chops into the pot and cook them for 4-minutes.
2. Cook and brown the chops in batches and set aside on a plate.
3. Add your onions, pears, into your instant pot and let them cook for 3-minutes or until lightly browned.
4. Add the cider and stir in the allspice and pepper sauce. Set the chops into the sauce. Close and secure the pot lid, set to Manual mode, and cook on high for a cook time of 10-minutes.
5. When the cook time is completed, release the pressure using quick-release. Serve warm.

Nutritional Information:

Calories: 318, Fat: 19g, Carbs: 4g, Protein: 31g

Instant Pot Pork Ragu

Servings: 4

Ingredients:

- 18 oz. pork tenderloin
- Salt and black pepper
- 1 tbsp. freshly chopped parsley, divided
- 2 bay leaves
- 2 sprigs of thyme
- 1 jar roasted red peppers
- 28 oz. crushed tomatoes
- 5 cloves garlic
- 1 tsp. olive oil

Directions:

1. Set your instant pot to the sauté mode, add the ghee to the pot and heat it.
2. Add the garlic to pot and sauté for 1-minute. Remove the garlic with a slotted spoon.
3. Place the pork into the pot and brown for 2-minutes per side. Add the remaining ingredients, make sure to leave half of your parsley for later use. Shut the pot lid and set to Manual mode, on high with a cook time of 45-minutes.
4. When the cook time is completed, release the pressure naturally over 10 minutes and discard the bay leaves.
5. Remove the pork and shred it and garnish with parsley. Serve warm.

Nutritional Information:

Calories: 93, Fat: 1.5 g, Carbs: 6 g, Protein: 8g

Vegetables and Vegan

Greek-Style Rice Salad

Servings: 4

Ingredients:

- 1¾ c. jasmine rice
- 1/3 c. Greek olives, pitted and halved
- ½ c. cucumber, cored and diced
- 1 c. lettuce, sliced
- 1 c. cherry tomatoes, diced
- 2¼ c. water
- Salt and white pepper
- ½ c. red onions, chopped
- ½ c. bell peppers, sliced
- 1 c. Greek-style cheese, crumbled

Directions:

1. Add water to an instant pot and stir in the rice.
2. Close the lid to pot and set it on BEANS/CHILI setting for 10-minute cook time.
3. When the cook time is completed, release the pressure using quick-release.
4. Add the rest of the ingredients into pot and mix. Serve chilled.

Nutritional Information:

Calories: 412, Fat: 7.7g, Carbs: 32g, Protein: 14.6g

Cheesy Creamed Broccoli & Potato Soup

Servings: 6

Ingredients:

- ½ c. celery stalk, finely chopped
- 1/3 tsp. ground black pepper
- 1 tsp. marjoram, dried
- 1 tsp. cayenne pepper
- 1/3 tsp. sea salt
- 3 oz. Parmigiano-Reggiano cheese, grated
- 1 cup leeks, chopped
- 1 lb. broccoli, chopped into florets
- 1 sliced carrot
- 3 Russet potatoes, peeled and diced
- 3½ c. vegetable broth

Directions:

1. Add all the ingredients (except cheese) into your instant pot.
2. Set the pot on the SOUP setting with a cook time of 25-minutes. When the cook time is completed, release the pressure using quick-release.
3. Using an immersion blender puree the soup.
4. Serve soup topped with grated cheese. Serve warm.

Nutritional Information:

Calories: 185, Fat: 4.3g, Carbs: 27.1g, Protein: 11.7g

Quinoa with Acorn Squash & Swiss Chard

Servings: 4

Ingredients:

- ¾ c. canned acorn squash puree
- ½ tbsp. Moroccan seasoning
- 1¾ c. uncooked quinoa, well rinsed
- ½ tsp. sea salt
- 2½ c. water
- ¼ tsp. ground allspice
- 1½ c. Swiss chard, trimmed and torn into pieces

Directions:

1. Throw all the ingredients into pot except for the Swiss chard.
2. Set the pot to Manual mode, on high, with a cook time of 5-minutes.
3. When the cook time is completed, release the pressure using quick-release.
4. Add the Swiss chard and stir, serve right away.

Nutritional Information:

Calories: 281, Fat: 4.6g, Carbs: 23g, Protein: 12.1g

Red Cabbage & Pear Delight

Servings: 4

Ingredients:

- 1 lb. red cabbage, shredded and stems removed
- 1¼ c. roasted vegetable stock
- ¼ tsp. freshly grated nutmeg
- 1 c. bosc pears, peeled, cored, diced
- A slurry (1½ tbsps. cornstarch dissolved in 4 tbsps. water)
- 3 tsps. ghee, room temperature
- ½ c. shallots, peeled, diced
- ½ tsp. Truvia
- Salt and black pepper
- ¾ c. white win

Directions:

1. Set your instant pot to the sauté mode, add the ghee.
2. Sauté the pears and shallots for 10-minutes. Add rest of the ingredients, except the cornstarch slurry.
3. Select the BEANS/CHILI setting with a cook time of 13-minutes. When the cook time is completed, release the pressure using quick-release.
4. Remove the lid of the pot and stir adding in the cornstarch slurry. Set the pot on sauté mode for 6-minutes to thicken the sauce. Serve warm.

Nutritional Information:

Calories: 147, Fat: 3.5g, Carbs: 20.9g, Protein: 3.2g

Creamed Root Vegetable Soup

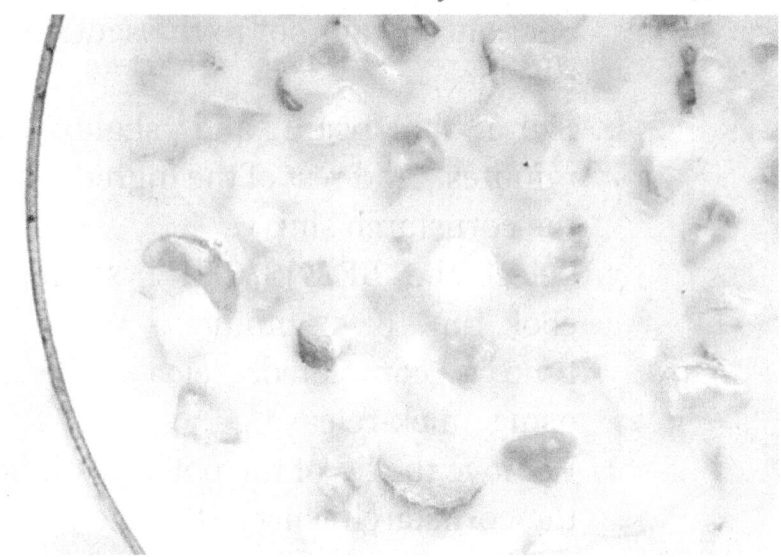

Servings: 8

Ingredients:

- ½ stick butter
- ½ c. chopped carrot
- ½ round Russet potato, peeled and cubed
- ½ lb. Yukon potatoes, peeled and cubed
- 1 c. chopped winter squash
- 3 c. water
- ½ c. chopped parsnip
- 1 c. chopped shallots
- 2 chopped celery ribs
- 1 tsp. dried dill weed
- 20 oz. canned evaporated milk
- Salt and black pepper
- ½ tsp. crushed red pepper flakes

Directions:

1. Add the potatoes, celery, winter squash, carrot, shallots, and parsnip to instant pot. Pour in water to the pot. Cover pot with lid.
2. Set the pot to the SOUP mode with a cook time of 20-minutes.
3. When the cook time is completed, release the pressure with quick-release.
4. Add the milk, butter, dill, salt, ground black pepper and simmer the soup for about 13-minutes on sautė mode. Serve hot.

Nutritional Information:

Calories: 259, Fat: 13g, Carbs: 28.8g, Protein: 8.7g

Cheesy Broccoli & Sweet Potato Soup

Servings: 4

Ingredients:

- 1 lb. broccoli head, broken florets
- 9 sweet potatoes, peeled and cut into 1/2 - inch cubes
- ½ c. white onions, peeled and sliced
- 3½ c. vegetable broth
- ¾ c. sharp Swiss cheese, shredded
- ¼ tsp. freshly ground black pepper
- 3 tsps. canola oil
- ½ tsp. kosher salt
- ¾ c. half-and-half
- 1 tsp. garlic, smashed

Directions:

1. Set your instant pot to the sauté mode, add the oil.
2. Add onion and garlic and cook for 5-minutes.
3. Add the broccoli, sweet potatoes, vegetable broth. Season with salt and pepper.
4. Close the lid to the pot. Select the BEANS/CHILI mode and a cook time of 6-minutes on high.
5. When the cook time is completed, release the pressure using the quick-release. Add the half-and-half and ½ cup shredded Swiss cheese.
6. Blend soup using an immersion blender. Serve soup hot and topped with remaining shredded cheese.

Nutritional Information:

Calories: 398, Fat: 18.7g, Carbs: 32.1g, Protein: 16.5g

Servings: 6

Ingredients:

- 3 c. toasted loaf Italian Bread, sliced
- 2 fresh rosemary sprigs
- ½ tsp. kosher salt
- 2 fresh thyme sprigs
- ¼ tsp. freshly ground black pepper
- 1¼ c. Comté cheese, grated
- 6½ c. chicken broth
- ½ stick butter
- 1/3 c. dry white wine
- ¾ tsp. granulated garlic
- 2¼ lbs. leeks, thinly sliced
- 1 tsp. Truvia

Directions:

1. Set your instant pot to the sautè mode, add the ghee.
2. Sautè the leeks in the pot for about 13-minutes. Add the salt, black pepper, and Truvia and stir often.
3. Add the wine then pour in the broth and stir to combine. Add the granulated garlic, thyme, and rosemary.
4. Close the pot lid and set it to the BEAN/CHILI mode on high, with a cook time of 8-minutes. Preheat oven to broil.
5. Ladle the soup into oven-proof bowls; top with toasted bread and grated cheese; place under broiler for about 9-minutes.

Nutritional Information:

Calories: 376, Fat: 16g, Carbs: 31.2g, Protein: 17.2g

Cheesy Leek and Kale Quiche

Servings: 6

Ingredients:

- 1 c. leeks, thinly sliced
- 3½ c. freshly chopped kale
- 1 tsp. cayenne pepper
- 1/3 tsp. ground black pepper
- ½ tsp. sea salt
- 1/3 c. grated Monterey-Jack cheese
- ¾ c. milk
- ¾ c. diced tomatoes
- 10 eggs

Directions:

1. Place a trivet inside of your instant pot and pour 1 ½ cups of water into the pot.
2. In large bowl whisk eggs, salt, cayenne pepper, black pepper, and milk. In a baking dish, combine the kale tomatoes, and leeks; stir to combine.
3. Pour the egg mixture over the kale mixture; stir to combine. Top with cheese.
4. Close the pot lid and set the pot to Manual mode, on high, with a cook time of 25-minutes.
5. When the cook time is completed, release the pressure using quick-release. Serve warm.

Nutritional Information:

Calories: 178, Fat: 10.1g, Carbs: 9.2g, Protein: 13.4g

Sweet Potato Spinach Curry with Chickpeas

Servings: 2

Ingredients:

- 1 small can drained chickpeas
- 1 tsp. coriander powder
- 1 tsp. olive oil
- ½-inch chopped ginger
- ½ chopped red onion
- 2 chopped tomatoes
- 2 c. freshly chopped spinach
- 3 chopped garlic cloves
- 1½ c. chopped sweet potatoes
- Squeeze of lemon
- Salt and pepper
- ¼ tsp. cinnamon
- ½ tsp. Garam Masala

Directions:

1. Set your instant pot on the sauté mode, add the oil and heat.
2. Add onions, ginger, and garlic for 3-minutes.
3. Add the spices, tomatoes and stir to mix and coat everything. Add the sweet potatoes, chickpeas, 1 ½ cups water, a dash of salt.
4. Close the pot lid and set to Manual mode, on high, with a cook time of 10-minutes.
5. When the cook time is completed, release the pressure using quick-release. Add the spinach and stir. Serve with a squirt of fresh lemon.

Nutritional Information:

Calories: 282, Fat: 11.2g, Carbs: 13g, Protein: 16.2g

Fish and Seafood

Coconut Fish Curry

Servings: 4

Ingredients:

- 1 lb. sea bass/cod cut into 1-inch pieces
- 3 lime wedges
- ¼ c. freshly chopped cilantro
- ½ tsp. white pepper
- ½ tsp. sea salt
- 1 tsp. ground ginger
- 1 tsp. ground turmeric
- 2 minced garlic cloves
- 2 tsps. Sriracha
- 1 tsp. date paste
- 1 tsp. coconut Aminos
- 1 tsp. fish sauce
- 1 tbsp. red curry paste
- 1 can coconut milk
- Juice of lime

Directions:

1. In a large bowl add lime juice, coconut milk, red curry paste, fish sauce, date paste, garlic, Sriracha, Coconut Aminos, ginger, turmeric, white pepper, sea salt and mix well. Place the sea bass/cod at the bottom of your instant pot.
2. Add the coconut milk mixture over the fish and close the pot lid. Set pot to Manual mode, on high, with a cook time of 3-minutes.
3. When the cook time is completed, release the pressure using quick-release.
4. Transfer to serving bowls and garnish with chopped cilantro. Serve warm.

Nutritional Information:

Calories: 276, Fat: 21g, Carbs: 4g, Protein: 18g

Salmon with Tomato Sauce

Servings: 3

Ingredients:

- 6 salmon fillets
- Black pepper and sea salt
- 1 tsp. dried parsley
- 1 tsp. dried oregano
- 1 tbsp. coconut oil
- 1.5 c. tomatillo sauce
- 1 chopped and seeded red pepper
- 1 tbsp. apple cider vinegar
- ¼ c. freshly chopped cilantro
- Feta

Directions:

1. Season the fish fillets with salt, pepper, vinegar, oregano, parsley and marinate for 2-hours.
2. Set your instant pot to the sautė mode, add the oil. Add fish fillets and cook for 1-minute on each side.
3. Set the pot to Manual mode, on high, with a cook time of 10-minutes.
4. When the cook time is completed, release the pressure using the quick-release.
5. Garnish with fresh chopped cilantro before serving.

Nutritional Information:

Calories: 284, Fat: 11g, Carbs: 7g, Protein: 22g

Tilapia Instant Pot Curry

Servings: 4

Ingredients:

- 1 lb. tilapia fillets cut into 2-inch pieces
- 1 tbsp. olive oil
- 1 tsp. sea salt
- ½ sliced yellow pepper
- ½ sliced green pepper
- ½ sliced onion
- 15-pieces curry leaves
- 1 tbsp. ginger garlic paste
- 1 can coconut milk
- ½ tsp. mustard seed
- ½ tsp. lime juice
- 8-mint leaves
- 3 sprigs cilantro
- ½ tsp. Garam Masala
- 1 tsp. cumin powder
- 2 tsps. coriander powder
- ½ tsp. red chili powder
- ½ tsp. turmeric powder

Directions:

1. Cut up the tilapia into 2-inch pieces.
2. Slice up the peppers, onion, and set your instant pot to the sauté mode, add the oil.
3. Add the mustard seeds to pot and allow it to splutter, add garlic paste and curry leaves and sauté for 30-seconds.
4. Add the sliced-up onions and bell peppers along with spices and stir for 30-seconds.
5. Add the coconut milk and bring to a simmer. Add the tilapia along with a few sprigs of cilantro and mix well.
6. Add a few mint leaves and close the lid of pot. Set on Manual mode, on high, with a cook time of 3-minutes.
7. When the cook time is completed, release the pressure using the quick-release. Serve warm.

Nutritional Information:

Calories: 280, Fat: 19g, Carbs: 4g, Protein: 24g

Poultry

Chicken & Tomato Soup

Servings: 6

Ingredients:

- 1 tbsp. olive oil
- Black pepper
- Salt
- 15 oz. chicken broth
- 15 oz. diced tomatoes
- 1 tsp. dried oregano
- 1 tsp. dried thyme
- 1 tbsp. minced garlic
- 1 chopped onion
- 1 lb. lean ground chicken

Directions:

1. Set your instant pot to the sauté mode, add the oil and heat it.
2. Cook chicken until the meat turns brown.
3. Add onion, thyme, garlic, and oregano and cook for 3-minutes. Add the tomatoes and chicken broth and close the pot lid.
4. Set the pot on the SOUP mode and cook for 30-minutes.
5. When the cooking is completed, release the pressure using the quick-release. Serve soup warm.

Nutritional Information:

Calories: 287, Fat: 11g, Carbs: 6g, Protein: 26g

Chicken Curry with Lemon & Coconut

Servings: 6

Ingredients:

- 1 can coconut milk
- ¼ c. lemon juice
- 1 tsp. lemon zest
- 4 lb. chicken breast
- ½ tsp. salt
- 1 tsp. turmeric

Directions:

1. In a bowl add lemon juice, the liquid portion of coconut milk, lemon zest and all the spices to make the marinade mixture.
2. Coat the chicken pieces with the mixture and then set aside.
3. Pour half the portion of coconut milk into an instant pot, add marinated chicken to pot.
4. Pour remaining coconut milk over chicken and close the lid to the pot. Set to the POULTRY setting and cook for 20-minutes.
5. When the cook time is completed, release the pressure using the quick-release. Serve the chicken warm as a side dish.

Nutritional Information:

Calories: 289, Fat: 13g, Carbs: 9g, Protein: 29g

Chicken Drumsticks in Tomato Sauce

Servings: 3

Ingredients:

- 6 chicken drumsticks
- 1 tbsp. cider vinegar
- 1.5 c. tomatillo sauce
- 1 tsp. olive oil
- 1 tsp. dried oregano
- 1/8 tsp. black pepper
- 1 tsp. salt
- ¼ c. chopped cilantro
- 1 jalapeno, halved and seeded

Directions:

1. Season the chicken with salt, vinegar, pepper, oregano and marinate them for 2-hours.
2. Set your instant pot to the sauté mode, add the oil and heat it.
3. Saute the chicken until the meat is browned.
4. After frying the chicken, add all the other ingredients (except for the cilantro) and shut the lid to the pot. Set on Manual mode on high, with a cook time of 20-minutes.
5. When the cook time is completed, release the pressure using quick-release. Garnish with chopped cilantro just before serving.

Nutritional Information:

Calories: 302, Fat: 13g, Carbs: 10g, Protein: 32g

Chicken Meatballs

Servings: 8

Ingredients:

- 1.5 lbs. ground chicken
- ¾ c. almond meal
- Chopped green onions
- 4 tbsps. butter
- 6 tbsps. hot sauce
- 2 tbsps. ghee
- 2 sliced green onions
- 2 minced garlic cloves
- Sea salt

Directions:

1. Add to mixing bowl almond meal, chicken, salt, garlic and green onion and mix well.
2. Shape mix into small meatballs. Heat the ghee in the instant pot in the sauté mode.
3. Cook the meatballs until they turn brown and are well-cooked. Take meatballs out of the pot and set them aside.
4. Add remaining ingredients into a bowl to make the sauce, add sauce to the pot and stir, add meatballs back into the pot.
5. Close the lid of the pot, set to Manual, on high, with a cook time of 20-minutes.
6. When the cook time is completed, release the pressure using the quick-release. Serve warm as a side dish.

Nutritional Information:

Calories: 305, Fat: 15g, Carbs: 12g, Protein: 32g

Green Curry Chicken

Servings: 4

Ingredients:

- 1.5 lbs. skinless chicken thighs
- 1 diced sweet potato
- 14 oz. coconut milk
- 1 tsp. sea salt
- 1 tbsp. coconut palm sugar
- 2 tbsps. green curry paste
- 1 sliced onion
- 3 diced zucchinis
- 2 tbsps. coconut oil
- Chopped cilantro
- Lime wedges

Directions:

1. Turn the instant pot onto the sauté mode, add 1 tablespoon coconut oil and heat it. Add zucchini and sauté for 8-minutes.
2. Make sure that the zucchini is brown and tender. Remove it from the pot and set aside.
3. Add remaining oil to the pot and cook onion on sauté mode for 5-minutes.
4. Add curry paste, salt, coconut sugar and cook for some time. Add the coconut milk and stir.
5. When it starts to steam, add the sweet potatoes and chicken and close the lid to the pot.
6. Set on Manual mode, on high, with a cook time of 10-minutes.
7. When the cook time is completed, release the pressure using quick-release.
8. Add the cooked zucchini and chopped cilantro and serve with lime wedges.

Nutritional Information:

Calories: 302, Fat: 13g, Carbs: 10g, Protein: 29g

Balsamic Chicken

Servings: 4

Ingredients:

- 2 lbs. chicken thigh, skinless and boneless
- Salt
- Pepper
- ½ tbsp. rosemary
- ½ tbsp. garlic powder
- 1 tbsps. coconut Aminos
- 1 tbsp. Worcestershire sauce
- 3 tbsps. Balsamic vinegar
- 1 c. cranberry sauce
- 1 chopped red onion
- 1 tbsps. cornstarch

Directions:

1. Spray the inside of instant pot with cooking spray.
2. Set the pot to the sauté mode. Season chicken thighs with pepper and salt then transfer to instant pot.
3. Brown the thighs for about 5-minutes. Add chopped up red onion to pot and sauté until caramelized.
4. Add ¼ cup water to pot. In a small mixing bowl add balsamic vinegar, cranberry sauce, coconut Aminos, rosemary, Worcestershire sauce, garlic powder and give it a nice mix.
5. Close the pot lid, set to Manual mode, on high, for a cook time of 15-minutes.
6. When the cook time is completed, release the pressure using the quick-release.
7. Remove the chicken from pot.
8. Add a mixture of 1 tablespoon of water and 1 tablespoon of cornstarch to the sauce in pot. Sauté for 3-minutes then pour gravy over the thighs and serve warm.

Nutritional Information:

Calories: 421, Fat: 7g, Carbs: 12g, Protein: 30g

Desserts

Chocolate cheesecake

Servings: 8

Ingredients:

- 2 eggs
- 4 egg yolks
- 1 c. sugar
- 3 c. cream cheese
- 2 tbsps. cocoa powder
- 1 tsp. vanilla sugar
- 1 c. almond flour
- 1 tbsp. butter
- 1 tbsp. sour cream
- 5 tbsp. butter
- 10 oz. biscuit
- 1 tsp. vanilla extract

Directions:

1. Crush the biscuits and put them in the blender.
2. Add the butter and blend the mixture well.
3. After this, take the instant pot pie form and put the blended crust there.
4. Flatten it well to get the homogenous layer.
5. Then combine the egg yolks and eggs together in the bowl.
6. Add the sugar and start to blend the mixture.
7. Add cream cheese and vanilla sugar.
8. After this, add the cocoa powder, almond flour, 1 tablespoon of butter, sour cream, and vanilla extract.
9. Blend the mixture well till it is smooth.
10. After this, pour the cream cheese mixture in the form with the crust.
11. Put the cheesecake in the instant pot vessel and close the lid.
12. Cook the dish at the pressure mode for 15 minutes.
13. When the cheesecake is cooked – remove it from the instant pot.
14. Put the form on the cheesecake in the ice bath and leave it for 10 minutes.
15. Then discard the cheesecake from the form.

16.Serve it immediately.

Nutritional Information:

calories 577, fat 43.4g, carbs 36.27g, protein 13g

Pistachio cookies

Servings: 8

Ingredients:

- 1 c. pistachio
- 4 tbsps. butter
- ½ tsp. baking soda
- 1 tsp. apple cider vinegar
- ½ c. brown sugar
- 1 egg
- 2 c. flour
- ¼ tsp. salt

Directions:

1. Combine the beaten egg with the brown sugar and whisk the mixture well.
2. Melt the butter and start to add it gradually to the egg-sugar mixture.
3. After this, add baking soda, apple cider vinegar, salt, and flour.
4. Knead the non-sticky dough.
5. Crush the pistachios well.
6. Then make the log from the dough and sprinkle it well with the crushed pistachio.
7. Cut the log into the cookies.
8. Put the cookies in the instant pot vessel.
9. Close the lid and cook the dish for 15 minutes at the pressure mode.
10. Chill the pistachio cookies very well.
11. Serve the dish immediately.
12. Enjoy!

Nutritional Information:

calories 320, fat 14.3g, carbs 41.77g, protein 8g

Aromatic lemon cake

Servings: 8

Ingredients:

- 3 eggs
- 1 c. sugar
- 1 c. flour
- 1 tsp. baking powder
- 5 tbsps. lemon juice
- 1 egg white
- 3 tbsps. sugar
- 1 tbsp. lemon zest
- 3 tbsps. butter
- 1 tsp. vanilla extract
- ½ tsp. salt
- ¼ tsp. ground cardamom

Directions:

1. Beat the eggs in the bowl and mix them with the help of the hand mixer.
2. When you get smooth mass – add the sugar and continue to mix the mass till you get lemon color.
3. Then add baking soda, lemon juice, and the lemon zest.
4. After this, add vanilla extract, salt, ground cardamom, and flour.
5. Take the spatula and churn the mixture till you get the lemon color soft dough.
6. Pour the lemon dough in the cake form.
7. Cook the cake for 30 minutes in the pressure mode.
8. Then chill the cake well and discard it from the form.
9. Whisk the egg white till the strong peaks.
10. Then add sugar and continue to whisk till sugar is dissolved – the icing is cooked.
11. After this, spread the cake with the icing.
12. Let the cake chill well.
13. Cut it into pieces.
14. Serve it.

Nutritional Information:

calories 211, fat 8.1g, carbs 28.99g, protein 6g

Conclusion

I sincerely hope that you have enjoyed reading this recipe book, as much as I have enjoyed writing it. I am confident that my recipe collection will offer you some new and healthy options to add to your daily diet. The best thing that I discovered while writing this book is that your meals do not have to be tasteless and boring to be healthy. I wish you immense success in adding new and healthier meal choices to your diet—that is not only good for you but taste delightful!

Peter Bragg

Made in the USA
Middletown, DE
24 November 2019

79253580R00129